T0178735

Artificial Intelligence and Big Data

Advances in Information Systems Set

coordinated by
Camille Rosenthal-Sabroux

Volume 8

Artificial Intelligence and Big Data

The Birth of a New Intelligence

Fernando Iafrate

WILEY

First published 2018 in Great Britain and the United States by ISTE Ltd and John Wiley & Sons, Inc.

ISTE Ltd
27-37 St George's Road
London SW19 4EU
UK

www.iste.co.uk

John Wiley & Sons, Inc.
111 River Street
Hoboken, NJ 07030
USA

www.wiley.com

Library of Congress Control Number: 2017961949

British Library Cataloguing-in-Publication Data
A CIP record for this book is available from the British Library
ISBN 978-1-78630-083-6

Contents

List of Figures

Preface

This book follows on from a previous book, *From Big Data to Smart Data* [IAF 15], for which the original French title contained a subtitle: "For a connected world". Today, we could add "without latency" to this title, as time has become the key word; it all revolves around acting faster and better than competitors in the digital environment, where information travels through the Internet at light speed.

Today more than ever before, time represents an "immaterial asset" with such a high added value (high-frequency trading operated by banks is an obvious example, I invite you to read Michael Lewis' book, Flash Boys: A Wall Street Revolt[1] [LEW 14]). It seems obvious that a large part of our decisions and subsequent actions (personal or professional) are dependent on the digital world (which mixes information and algorithms for processing this information); imagine spending a day without your laptop, smartphone or tablet, and you will see the extent to which we have organized our lives around this "Digital Intelligence". Although it does render us many services and

---

1 This book by Michael Lewis looks at the ins and outs of high-frequency trading (HFT): its history, means used, the stakes involved and so on.

increases our autonomy, it also accentuates our dependence and even addiction to these technologies (what a paradox!). This "new" world is structured around the Internet and requires companies to make decisions and act in a highly competitive environment, managing complex data in a matter of milliseconds (or less).

We live in a world where "customer experience" has become the key and our demand as consumers (for all types of goods, services or content: messaging, products, offers, information) is only growing. We demand to be "processed" in a relevant way, even as we navigate in this digital world "anonymously" (without formerly having used a personal authenticated account), which implies that other mechanisms must be in place to allow this "traceability". Who was it who said that "the habit does not make the monk"? I fear that in this digitized world, our clothes in the Internet are the traces we leave (navigation, cookies, IP address, download history, etc.), voluntarily or not, allowing a digital identity to be built without our knowledge and therefore being one that we barely or do not have any control over!

All this information is interconnected, joined together as they are being generated, following the "keyring" principle (see Figure 1). They are then exploited by targeting, segmenting and through recommendation engine solutions, which have been implemented over the last decade or so and are based on software agents backed by rule engines (recommendation engines). In order to meet a contact's expectation of "relevance", "a company does not own a customer but merely the time that he chooses to devote". During this time, which becomes the "grail" for companies to unveil vaults of imaginative ideas (but also much spending in terms of finances) to attract customers to their channels (website, call center, shops, etc.), they must be as "relevant" as possible.

The solutions currently in place (rule/recommendation engine) are not very interactive with their environment (they are predefined models based on a limited number of descriptive variables for the situation), they do not exhibit much self-learning (updating of models after analytical processing, which is often very arduous) and the result is that the same causes (identified by a few variables) trigger the same effects. These solutions do not or take very little account of context variations in real time (how a user arrived on a web page, what content they saw just before, what the nature of their search is, etc.), or do they consider results from previous decisions and actions. Last but not least, they barely or do not allow all contextual data to be exploited (navigation behavior, what was previously proposed in terms of content, the resulting actions, etc.).

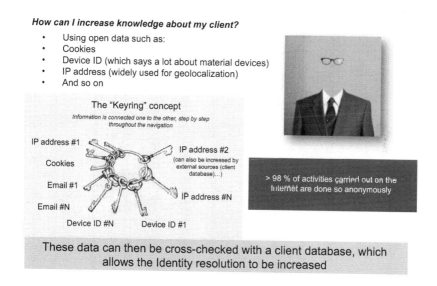

Figure 1. *Identity resolution*

This need to act and react in real time in a complex environment has been the case for years, and the advent of

Big Data and connected devices has only increased the complexity of processing this information; solutions and organizations (statisticians, decision analysts, etc.) are overwhelmed by this continuous flow of data (the Internet never sleeps). No or few solutions have been proposed through processes and historical analysis tools in companies, which tend to be too cumbersome and complex to develop, and require resources to be implemented despite that these resources are becoming increasingly scarce (it is likely to be one of the major problems over the next few years in this field – the lack of Business Intelligence experts and statisticians will be very much highlighted). Consumer purchasing behaviors are constantly changing (collaborative platforms such as Uber and Airbnb have "invented" this new business model), which will ultimately create new risks (for those who cannot adapt to this ever-changing world) and opportunities (for those who will be able to exploit this new "Eldorado" that is "Big Data").

Artificial Intelligence (AI) is one of the most promising solutions to the massive, self-learning, autonomous exploitation of "Big Data". More precisely, "Deep Learning", which emerged in the 1980s with the advent of neural networks, is now becoming the keystone to this new generation of solutions. Advances in technology with digitized data flows have opened up new horizons in this field and anything that has not misled the major technological players in Business Intelligence has been swallowed up as the logical sequel to Big Data.

There are many possible fields of application for AI, such as robotics (connected and autonomous cars), home automation (smart home), health (assistance in medical diagnosis), security, personal assistants (which will become essential tools in our daily lives), expert systems, image, sound and facial recognition (and why not analyze emotions too), natural language processing... But also, customer relations management (to anticipate or even exceed our expectations). All these systems will be self-learning, their knowledge will only grow with time and they will be able to exchange knowledge between each other.

Certain people like Bill Gates, the founder of Microsoft, or serial entrepreneur Elon Musk, or Steve Wozniak, co-founder of Apple, or scientist Stephen Hawking were deeply moved by the thought that AI could change within our society, at the risk that humanity could one day be controlled by machines (somewhat reminiscent of the film "The Matrix"). The purpose of this book is not to be philosophical or ethical (although this would be an interesting – and necessary – debate, as the questions it raises are relevant). What can be seen throughout human history is that technological development has always occurred alongside evolution, for the "better" and for the "worse". I will therefore focus on the role (current and in the near future) of AI in the world of Business Intelligence, how AI could replace (supplement) Business Intelligence as we know it today now companies are beginning to adopt solutions built around AI platforms, and how these solutions will help create bridges between "traditional" and Big Data Business Intelligence.

There are two types of AI: strong AI and weak AI.

Strong AI refers to a machine that can produce intelligent behavior[2] and maintain an impression of real self-consciousness, true emotion. In this world, the machine can understand what it does (and therefore the consequences of its actions). Intelligence arises from the biology of the brain based on a process of learning and reasoning (thus it is material and follows an "algorithmic" logic). In this regard,

---

2 This is further elaborated in Chapter 1.

scientists do not see any limits to one day being able to achieve machine intelligence (or an equivalent material element) in theory, a machine with a certain consciousness, one that could have emotions. This topic, as you may have read just before, is the subject of much debate. If today we do not yet have computers or robots that are as intelligent as humans, it is not due to a hardware problem but rather a problem of design. Therefore, we can consider that there is no functional limitation. In order to determine whether a machine can be considered as having strong AI or not, it must pass the Turing test.[3]

Weak AI consists of implementing increasingly autonomous, self-learning systems with algorithms that can solve problems of a certain class. But in this case, the machine acts as if it were intelligent, but it is more of a "simulation" of human intelligence based on learning (supervised or not). We can teach machines to recognize sounds and images from a database that represents the type of learning expected (such as recognizing a car in a batch of images, for example) – this is supervised learning. The machine can discover by itself the elements it analyzes, up to naming them. In the example of an image of a car, the machine analyzes the images that are proposed to it, and bit by bit (deep learning via neural networks) will learn by itself

3 From Wikipedia: "To demonstrate this approach, Turing proposes a test inspired by a party game, known as the "Imitation Game", in which a man and a woman go into separate rooms and guests try to tell them apart by writing a series of questions and reading the typewritten answers sent back. In this game, both the man and the woman aim to convince the guests that they are the other. [...] Turing described his new version of the game as follows: We now ask the question, "What will happen when a machine takes the part of A in this game?" Will the interrogator decide wrongly as often when the game is played like this as he does when the game is played between a man and a woman? These questions replace our original, "Can machines think?"".

to associate the concept of car to the analyzed images and, when one of the associated images is labeled as a car, it will know how to "verbalize" it – this is non-supervised learning.

Fernando IAFRATE
December 2017

Introduction

I.1. The "fully" digital era is upon us, can we still escape it?

Nothing has ever been less certain. Seeing the exponential speed with which we have embraced digital technologies, we have probably never seen anything like it in history (each new generation accelerates this movement). Its impact on our societies will be at least as significant as Gutenberg's invention of printing in 1450 (which enabled books to exist, thus linking together knowledge, cultures, ideas, etc.). Would we have developed so quickly without printing? One can only take a step back and observe this frenetic digitization of our world, where reality and virtual reality merge to create a more or less conscious "digital assimilation" model in which the Internet is the medium.

In its beginnings (basically before the year 2000 and the advent of blogs[1], social networks, etc.), the Internet was a medium that lay in the hands of companies and institutional stakeholders who were (in fact) "masters" of content, where

---

1 A blog is used to periodically and regularly publish articles that are usually succinct news reports on a given topic or profession.

the role of the Internet user was to consume this content in a rather passive way, with no or little interaction between the user and the Internet.

This communication model is also known as Web 1.0, as opposed to Web 2.0, which arose with the introduction of blogs (contraction of web logs) in the early 2000s. Blogs allowed a new mode of expression and sharing on the web, for which the evolution is mainly characterized by the contributory role of Internet users.

The wave of "open source"[2] is at the core of this "revolution". Open source is a concept created in 1982 by Richard Stallmann[3], which states that users are free to use a software, to make it evolve and publish it (and even distribute it) for free or not (any company or individual has the right to market it).

Blogs were one of the first (and probably the most significant) steps in the emergence of Web 2.0, quickly followed by others, such as tools for publishing digital content through wikis, sharing of photos, videos and finally, social networks like Facebook, Twitter and others (see Figure I.1). All of these have definitely and irreversibly changed our approach to the world and the global

---

2 Open Source, or "open source code", applies to software for which the license meets criteria specifically established by the Open Source Initiative, in other words the possibility of free redistribution, access to the source code and creation of derivative works. This source code is usually available to the general public and is the result of collaboration between programmers.

3 From Wikipedia: "Richard Matthew Stallman (born March 16, 1953), often known by his initials, rms, is an American software freedom activist and programmer. He campaigns for software to be distributed in a manner such that its users receive the freedoms to use, study, distribute and modify that software".

network that is the Internet. These changes have induced subsequent changes in behavior (consumption of goods or services) because of this huge marketplace that has become the Internet, where "everything" (and its opposite) is accessible in just a few clicks. Companies have had to integrate these changes in their approach to customer relations (higher customer volatility, less loyalty to a brand, easier comparison... competition is extremely tough on the Web). Customer relations are changing rapidly; the customer is no longer "owned" (in the marketing sense of the word) by a company, but rather it is the time that the Internet user is ready to devote to the company (via different contact channels) that is exploitable. This time has therefore become precious to companies, and they must be able to exploit it based on the time frame of the Internet user rather than that of the company (through "traditional" contact policies) in order to optimize this relationship.

Companies have understood this well, and those who can/will adapt most quickly to fill this "ecosystem" (we should really refer to it as "cyber space") will have a more secure future than others (welcome to digital Darwinism, where time to market and the ability to act quickly and well are the key to survival). The advent of the smartphone, as well as other devices such as tablets (and more recently, the iPhone, that was launched in 2007 but which seems to have always been there, such is how relevant it has proven itself to be), has allowed access to the Internet anywhere and at any time, which has only amplified this movement and contributed to the "digital assimilation" that has since become ever more widespread.

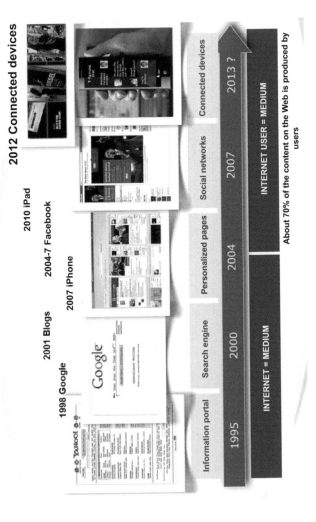

Figure I.1. *"Digital assimilation"*

The next steps in the evolution of this topic will undoubtedly be linked to connected devices and all the services they come with in fields such as health, transport, home automation, but also, the world of augmented reality through metadata (text, images, sounds, etc.), which will aim to "enrich" our vision of the world in real time: a world where reality and virtual reality will merge to the point of becoming one (a cyber space). There is a good chance (and the trend is already underway) that our smartphones will evolve toward "smart assistants", which will bring Artificial Intelligence software/algorithms into the mix. This software continuously learns about us (our behaviors, actions, preferences, shopping habits, social networks and more) to help us better manage our time, our actions... by anticipation (the word has been unleashed, and will undoubtedly be very significant). This will accentuate the need for security of our personal data to make sure we avoid going from "Big Data" to "Big Brother"!

I.2. How we are shifting from digital "unconsciousness" to digital "consciousness"?

Digital unconsciousness could be translated as: "I act in the digital world without worrying about my data being exploited by third parties". This situation occurs due to the fact that before the digitization of our world (basically, before the Internet), we were not (or were barely) confronted with this kind of problem. Our personal (digitized) data were only really available to administrations, institutions (such as banks or insurance companies) or even to certain companies to which we had given our consent ("opt-in") for commercial exploitation, all protected by law enforced by the CNIL[4]

---

4 The CNIL is responsible for ensuring that information technology is at the service of the citizen and does not infringe on human identity, human rights, privacy or individual or public freedoms.

(*Commission Nationale de l'Informatique et des Libertés*). In short, we felt "safe", and Web 1.0 did not fundamentally change this impression (data or traces that we left on the Internet were not exploited (much) because of faults in (technological) solutions and/or the cost was too high relative to the expected value). But that was not the end of it! The digitization of our world accelerated in the early 2000s, then the advent of social networks undermined this "belief" that we owned our own personal data and that we were protected against others using them (please take an interest in the terms and conditions for applications you download every day, you may be surprised!). The collection of personal data is very often linked to a free service offer (if you do not pay for a product or service, ultimately the product is you). The age of naivety is now over, we know that our personal data are subject to all kinds of analyses, and the technologies related to Big Data (mainly Hadoop) have made it possible to analyze these data; some state scandals (such as the PRISM[5] project, which has now paid the price by agitating the "webosphere") have only confirmed this.

Digital consciousness would therefore be "I understand that my actions in the digital world can be analyzed through my data". This awareness should not turn into a mistrust of the Internet and big players such as GAFA (Google, Amazon, Facebook and Apple – we could also add Microsoft) and others... But allowing ourselves to behave on the Internet in full knowledge of the facts ("is the game worth the risk?"), and to understand and know that we have become the center

---

5 PRISM, also known as US-984XN1, is a U.S. electronic surveillance program that collects information from the Internet and other electronic service providers. This classified program, under the National Security Agency (NSA), targets people living outside the United States.

of attention (when the Internet is "free", what we need to understand is that the "product" is the user). The real question should now be: can we escape? The answer is probably not! But the strengthening of legislations (April 2016) on the storage and use of personal data is on the agenda; Europe has voted[6] for the GDPR[7], which aims to give citizens control of their personal data.

With regard to the safeguards to be implemented, Article 32 lists some of the measures that could be used by companies:

– use of pseudonymization;

– data encryption;

– adoption of means to ensure confidentiality;

– integrity, availability and resilience of systems;

– adoption of measures to restore availability and access to personal data in the event of a technical or physical incident;

– regular verification of measures.

6 http://ec.europa.eu/justice/data-protection/reform/files/regulation_oj_en.pdf.
7 Wikipedia: "The General Data Protection Regulation (GDPR) (Regulation (EU) 2016/679) is a regulation by which the European Parliament, the Council of the European Union and the European Commission intend to strengthen and unify data protection for all individuals within the European Union (EU). It also addresses the export of personal data outside the EU. The GDPR aims primarily to give control back to citizens and residents over their personal data and to simplify the regulatory environment for international business by unifying the regulation within the EU. [...] The proposed new EU data protection regime extends the scope of the EU data protection law to all foreign companies processing data of EU residents".

I.3. The traces we leave on the Internet (whether voluntarily or not) constitute our Digital Identity

Digital identity must be understood as a virtual identity that gathers all the information (data) on the Internet that is about us (see Figure I.2). As in the real world, this identity is constantly evolving, representing different elements of our personality and how we are perceived. It is divided into two types:

– declarative identity, which is the data that we (or a third party) voluntarily enter (social networks, blogs, etc.);

– behavioral identity (downloading, browsing, cookies, etc.).

Each new connection, navigation or other activity on the Internet enriches this informational heritage about us, of which we are not the custodians. And therein lies the problem: we have in fact "delegated" the management of our identity to a third party (like search engines).

This identity ultimately becomes our e-reputation. One aspect of the digital identity, "name googling", is widely used (and not only by future employers) to find out who you are and get a first impression (and as we all know, "you never have a second chance to make a first impression"). In just a few clicks, this method allows an entity to check a person's profile (CV, professional network, what we say about them…) to evaluate their online influence (presence on forums, etc.), in short to get a more "accurate" idea about this person.

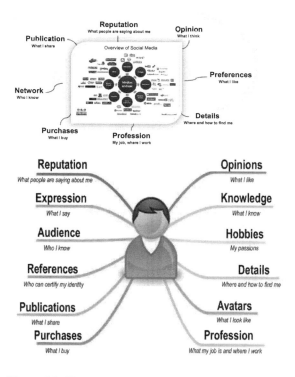

Figure I.2. *The traces we leave on the Internet (whether voluntarily or not) form our Digital Identity*

I.4. The digitization of our world continues, and connected devices are the next step (the Internet of Things)

While the Internet does not extend beyond the virtual world, the Internet of Things will allow for a bridge between the real and the virtual world through an exchange of information and data from "sensors" in the real world. The Internet of Things is expected to be the next evolution of the web, under the name Web 3.0[8], the web of things, whereas

---

8 From Wikipedia: "The Internet of Things (IoT) is the network of physical devices, vehicles and other items embedded with electronics, software, sensors, actuators and network connectivity, which enable these objects to collect and exchange data. The IoT allows objects to be sensed or controlled remotely across existing network infrastructure, creating opportunities for

Web 2.0[9] had more of a social approach (blogs, social networks, etc.). Connected devices will (exponentially) accentuate the volume of data exchanged and which is available on the Internet (some studies speak of 40 times more data by 2020) (see Figure I.3). Big Data and Artificial Intelligence will "feed" themselves and will allow the implementation of new services in fields of application as diverse as home automation, health, transport and more.

---

more direct integration of the physical world into computer-based systems, and resulting in improved efficiency, accuracy and economic benefit in addition to reduced human intervention. When IoT is augmented with sensors and actuators, the technology becomes an instance of the more general class of cyber-physical systems, which also encompasses technologies such as smart grids, virtual power plants, smart homes, intelligent transportation and smart cities. Each thing is uniquely identifiable through its embedded computing system but is able to interoperate within the existing Internet infrastructure. Experts estimate that the IoT will consist of about 30 billion objects by 2020. [...] As well as the expansion of Internet-connected automation into a plethora of new application areas, IoT is also expected to generate large amounts of data from diverse locations, with the consequent necessity for quick aggregation of the data, and an increase in the need to index, store and process such data more effectively".

9 From Wikipedia: "Web 2.0 refers to World Wide Web Websites that emphasize user-generated content, usability (ease of use, even by non-experts) and interoperability (this means that a Website can work well with other products, systems, and devices) for end users. [...] Web 2.0 does not refer to an update to any technical specification, but to changes in the way Web pages are designed and used. A Web 2.0 website may allow users to interact and collaborate with each other in a social media dialogue as creators of user-generated content in a virtual community, in contrast to the first generation of Web 1.0-era Websites where people were limited to the passive viewing of content. Examples of Web 2.0 features include social networking sites and social media sites (e.g., Facebook), blogs, wikis, folksonomies ("tagging" keywords on Websites and links), video sharing sites (e.g., YouTube), hosted services, Web applications ("apps"), collaborative consumption platforms and mashup applications".

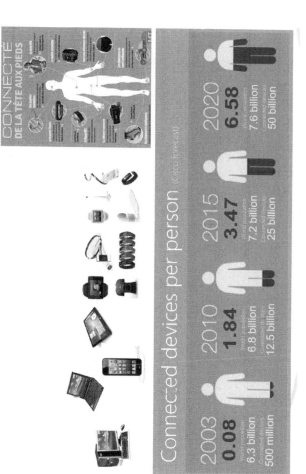

Figure I.3. *Number of connected devices per person by 2020*

This information, consisting of traces that we leave on the Internet (voluntarily or not), is an important part of what is now called "Big Data"[10]. They say a lot about us (and increasingly more so with the advent of connected devices), they are/will be the subject of increasingly accurate analyses and they are/will be the raw material for a new form of digital intelligence (Artificial Intelligence)[11].

The aim of this book is to take a small step back and consider how this phenomenon will change our analytical approach (mainly within a company in terms of knowledge of a "Client") to make it more dynamic, more reactive and learn more with the consequences of less "human" and more "machine". This trend has already begun: in the last decade, we have moved away from Customer Relationship Management (CRM[12]), where we had to have a 360° view of the customer, with an interconnection of web channels and call centers. It was a time when the reference point of a

---

10 Big Data designates data sets that become so voluminous, with various formats and at a high velocity, that it becomes impossible to process them through traditional database management or information management tools.

11 Artificial intelligence (AI) can be defined as the ability of a machine to perform functions that are normally associated with human intelligence: comprehension, reasoning, dialog, adaptation, learning...

12 From Wikipedia: "Customer relationship management (CRM) is an approach to managing a company's interaction with current and potential customers. It uses data analysis about customers' history with a company and to improve business relationships with customers, specifically focusing on customer retention and ultimately driving sales growth. One important aspect of the CRM approach is the systems of CRM that compile data from a range of different communication channels, including a company's Website, telephone, e-mail, live chat, marketing materials and, more recently, social media. Through the CRM approach and the systems used to facilitate it, businesses learn more about their target audiences and how to best cater to their needs. However, adopting the CRM approach may also occasionally lead to favoritism within an audience of consumers, resulting in dissatisfaction among customers and defeating the purpose of CRM".

customer was the home (mainly identified through postal address and household members: adults, children, seniors, etc.). Technological developments, such as the smartphone and social networks have changed the landscape such that we no longer contact a location (the home) but a person (in motion). We have shifted from a 360° approach to an approach that we could call "37.2°" (the average temperature of the human body). Personalization was born and it is drawing with it a new model of customer relationship that is based on capturing and analyzing all forms of interaction with the customer. Customer Experience Management (CXM[13]) goes beyond CRM in many aspects and these points will be further elaborated in Chapter 4.

---

13 In the early 1990s, CRM focused on how to capture, store and process client data. Now, CXM is an approach that integrates all processes and organizations in order to offer an individual service by placing customer expectations at the heart of the company's concerns. It is therefore imperative to involve all teams in the company and not just those dedicated to customer relations.

What is Intelligence?

Before we start discussing Business Intelligence (BI) and Artificial Intelligence (AI), let us begin by reviewing what we mean by "intelligence" (in a non-philosophical context).

1.1. Intelligence

ETYMOLOGY.– The word "intelligence" comes from the Latin *intelligentia* meaning "faculty of perception", "comprehension". It is derived from intellĕgĕre ("discern", "grasp", "understand"), which is composed of the prefix *inter-* ("between") and the verb lĕgĕre ("pick", "choose", "read"). Etymologically speaking, intelligence consists of making a choice, a selection.

We could therefore say that intelligence is defined as the set of mental faculties that make it possible to understand things and facts, and to discover the relationships between them in order to arrive at a rational understanding (knowledge) (as opposed to intuition). It makes it possible to understand and adapt to new situations and can therefore also be defined as adaptability. Intelligence can be seen as the ability to process information to achieve an objective. In this book, we are particularly interested in the latter definition: projecting intelligence in the digital world of the

Internet where information travels at the speed of light. Our digitalized world continuously generates information (the Internet never sleeps) and does so in various forms (transactions, texts, images, sounds, etc.), which is what we call "Big Data[1]". Since the dawn of time, "man seeks to know how to act" and he has used all the information at his disposal, learning from past experiences and using it to project himself into a more or less immediate future. The challenge for companies is to make this information "intelligent": intelligible, diffusible and understandable by those who will have to transform it into an action plan ("know how to act"), which is the fundamental principle of BI (see section 1.2 for more details).

1.2. Business Intelligence

BI could be defined as a data principle that is "augmented" by a certain amount of computer tools (database, dashboards, etc.) and know-how (data management, analytical processes, etc.). Its objective is to help "decision-makers" (both strategic and operational) in their decision-making and/or management of their activities. One of the most important principles of this is that operational decisions must be made as closely as possible to their implementation based on indicators that are directly linked to the operational processes they control. Their aim is to make the right decision at the right time (timing has become a key word in BI) in order to limit the risks of deceleration between the operational situation and the

---

1 Big Data are datasets that are so large they become difficult to process using traditional "classic" database management tools. The quantitative explosion and multiple formats of digital data (image, sound, transaction, text, etc.) require new ways of seeing and analyzing this digitized world. Big Data are characterized by Volume, Variety of format, Velocity (the Internet never sleeps) and Value (for those who know how to exploit them).

indicators that reflect it. BI platforms have had to adapt to this new situation. In the mid-2000s, this led to the creation of a new architecture called Operational BI[2]. This was aimed more at "field" players, in other words operational staff who managed their activities in near-real time, although BI had historically been more of a decision-making tool aimed at analysts and strategic decision makers (who are not at all or not very well "connected" to the field). On a technical level, BI consists of acquiring data from various sources (varied both in terms of content and form), processing it (cleaning, classifying, formatting, storing, etc.), analyzing it and then learning from it (scores, behavioral models, etc.). This will then feed into the management, decision-making and action processes within companies. It requires data management platforms (continued use of IT tools for processing and publishing data) and also an organization (BI competence center) that will be in charge of transforming these data into information and then into knowledge. These Business Intelligence Competency Centers (BICCs[3]) produce analyses, reports and business activity monitoring tables to inform decision makers, regardless of whether they are strategic or operational.

---

2 Operational BI differs from Business Intelligence due to two structural elements: (1) time taken (velocity) to update indicators (aligned with the time frame of the operational processes it controls), and (2) the granularity of implemented data (only those needed to feed operational management indicators), so in short, less but more frequent data.
3 A Business Intelligence Competence Center (BICC) is a multifunctional organizational team that has defined tasks, roles, responsibilities and processes to support and promote the effective use of Business Intelligence (BI) within an organization. A BICC coordinates activities and resources to ensure that an evidence-based approach is systematically considered throughout the organization. It is responsible for the governance structure of analytical programs and projects (solutions and technical architecture). It is also responsible for building plans, priorities, infrastructure and skills that enable the organization to make strategic, forward-looking decisions using BI and analytics software capabilities.

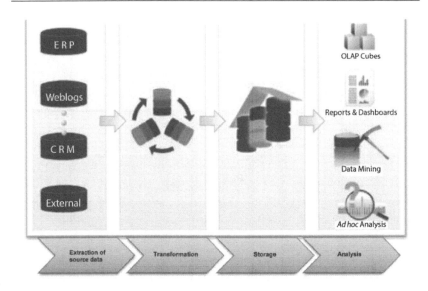

Figure 1.1. *Diagram showing the transformation of information into knowledge*

Companies (mainly large companies, given the costs associated with implementing such solutions and processes) have acquired real know-how in terms of data processing and its transformation into knowledge. They have equipped themselves and organized themselves around competence centers, the BICCs (often large vertical business units: Marketing & Sales, Finance, Logistics, HR, etc.) and are backed by tools available on the market (publishers of BI solutions are quite numerous). But it has to be said that the continuous flow of information generated in a world that is becoming more and more digital every day has become a real problem for companies (in the early 1990s, the world was producing less than 100 gigabytes[4] of data per second. By

4 1 Gigabyte = 1,000,000,000,000 bytes. 1 byte = 8 bits, and is used for encoding information; 1 bit is the simplest unit in a numbering system, which can only take two values (0 or 1). A bit or binary element can represent either a logical alternative, expressed as false and true, or a digit of the binary system.

2020, we will exceed 50,000 according to the IDC International Data Corporation). Companies are finding it increasingly difficult to cope with this continuous flow of information, as the time frame for decision-making and therefore ultimately for taking action in our connected world is now just milliseconds. The processes, tools and staff (which are increasingly scarce resources) required to run BI departments are no longer sufficient. Companies are forced to make choices (in terms of analysis, and/or the ability to interact in real time); however, "choosing is depriving oneself". The advent of connected devices is accelerating this "analytical rupture[5]", as BI must reinvent itself and find new ways to process these data. Perhaps Artificial Intelligence is part of the answer.

1.3. Artificial Intelligence

There are many definitions for Artificial Intelligence. Wikipedia has one too (which I will let you look up in your own time). In this book, and in order not to get lost along the way, we will focus solely on the "learning" dimension for decisions and actions. We will look at how Deep Learning and/or Machine Learning, which will be described in detail in the next section, are becoming more and more common in companies to complement existing BI tools and processes. The main advantage of Artificial Intelligence versus BI is undoubtedly its ability to analyze and make decisions in a few milliseconds within a context of very complex analyses. Its raw material is Big Data and it takes just a millisecond (or even less in some cases) to make a decision. Another advantage is its ability to learn, or the ability of Artificial Intelligence tools to learn from their experiences (analyses, decisions, actions): "there is no good or bad choice, there are

---

5 The company is overwhelmed by its "data". In general, less than 10 % of the data actually available to the company are formally analyzed and/or used in a decision-making process.

only experiences". This is how Artificial Intelligence approaches human intelligence, learning from experience and remembering it (one way or another). This digital memory, which gets enriched as different experiences occur and develop, will be the keystone of decision-making processes, and over time it will constitute the company's memory.

Thus, we refer to Tom Mitchell's (1997) definition of Machine Learning:

> A computer program is said to learn from experience E with respect to some class of tasks T and performance measure P if its performance at tasks in T, as measured by P, improves with experience E.

In other words, a self-learning process of decision-making and action is linked to one or more objectives to be achieved. The result of this decision/action will be measured relative to the objective and will be propagated back into the model in order to improve the probability that the decision/action will be able to achieve its objective (each new iteration will be seen as a new experience, which will enable the process to quickly adapt to changing situations).

1.4. How BI has developed

BI, like most disciplines with a strong adherence to technology, evolves with technological progress (of which there have been many in recent years). BI has experienced many of these in less than 20 years, which is summarized in Figure 1.2.

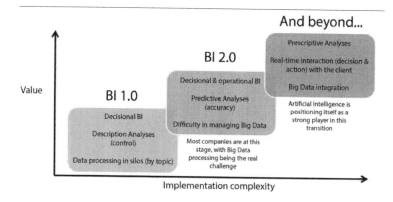

Figure 1.2. *Business Intelligence evolution cycle*

1.4.1. *BI 1.0*

In the late 1990s and early 2000s, companies organized themselves around BICCs to streamline and optimize their reporting activities. At this stage, BI was mainly decisional[6] and organized in silos (by subject such as marketing, logistics and finance). No or few management indicators (updated in "real time", or more precisely, aligned with the temporality of operational processes) were available for operational actors; this was still very much a world for experts, where BI (through its tools) had some difficulty in spreading itself throughout a company (for both technical and "political" reasons). Most of the solutions were subject-

---

6 Decisional Business Intelligence (in the context of BI 1.0) is mainly focused on large data processing, which can be lengthy. The volume of data to be processed and the analytical processing of these data take precedence over the timing (frequency of updating indicators, etc.). The "consumers" of this decisional BI are mainly analysts and/or managers, rarely operational staff (at least not in "real-time" monitoring and optimization of processes), because of a lack of "temporality" of the data (an activity-monitoring indicator that is only updated once a day [in the morning] for data on the previous day allows no or little operational optimization).

oriented, and data were organized and stored by type of activity (marketing data, HR data, financial data, etc.) with no or few possible crossovers between the different silos. The methods of analysis are said to be "descriptive", which involves drawing up a picture of a situation (for example managing a sales activity) as it appears subsequent to following the compilation and classification of data. It allows the data to be managed, monitored, classified, etc., but provides little or no information on situations to come.

1.4.2. *BI 2.0*

In the mid-2000s, operational needs became more prevalent, thus operational decision-makers saw the arrival of a new generation of tools that enabled them to manage and optimize their operational processes in real time: operational BI was born and with it, the temporality of information and its processing became the key point. BI platforms have been integrating more and more prediction functions, and BI has been becoming increasingly more democratic as communication technologies (tablets, smartphones) have evolved to allow access to information anytime and anywhere. These developments and the increase in the number of people connected to the Internet have multiplied the volumes and formats of data to be processed, and thus Big Data was born. Most companies are at this stage now, with Big Data management still being a real challenge for companies. The BI solutions in place are not well-adapted to the poorly structured data management of data produced on the Internet (images, videos, blogs, logs, etc.); their volume and velocity are additional difficulties on top of the formatting issue. Big Data are generally defined by four dimensions (the 4V):

– *Volume*: the Internet generates a continuous flow of all types of data, of which the volumes are growing exponentially (the Internet of Things will accelerate this growth even more), making it virtually impossible to process the data through existing BI solutions. New solutions are emerging (such as Hadoop[7] for massive data processing).

– *Velocity*: the Internet never sleeps, data arrive in a constant uninterrupted stream and it must be processed in near-real time if we want to extract the maximum value from it.

– *Variety*: Big Data are structured or unstructured data (text, data from sensors, sound, video, route data, log files, etc.). New knowledge is emerging from the collective analysis of these data.

– *Value*: Big Data are the new "gold mine" that all companies want to be able to use, and the rampant digitization of our world is increasing the value of these data every day.

1.4.2.1. *Hadoop platforms*

Hadoop platforms were launched by Google (in 2004) to process huge volumes of data (billions of requests are made

---

7 (From Wikipedia) Apache Hadoop is an open-source software framework used for distributed storage and processing of dataset of big data using the MapReduce programming model. It consists of computer clusters built from commodity hardware. All the modules in Hadoop are designed with a fundamental assumption that hardware failures are common occurrences and should be automatically handled by the framework.
The core of Apache Hadoop consists of a storage part, known as Hadoop Distributed File System (HDFS), and a processing part that is a MapReduce programming model. Hadoop splits files into large blocks and distributes them across nodes in a cluster. It then transfers packaged code into nodes to process the data in parallel. This approach takes advantage of data locality, where nodes manipulate the data they have access to. This allows the dataset to be processed faster and more efficiently than it would be in a more conventional supercomputer architecture that relies on a parallel file system where computation and data are distributed via high-speed networking.

every day on the Internet via search engines). It was inspired by the massive parallel processing solutions used for large scientific calculations. The principle was to parallelize the processing of data (MapReduce) by distributing them over hundreds (or even thousands) of servers (Hadoop Distributed File System) organized into processing nodes. Apache (open-source) embraced the concept and pushed it to evolve into what it is today. MapReduce is a set of processes for distributing data and processing it across a large number of servers (guaranteed by the "Map" process in order to ensure parallel processing). The results are then consolidated (guaranteed by the "Reduce" process) and fed into the analytical suite (Smart Data) where this information will be analyzed, consolidated, etc., in order to enrich the decision-making process (whether human or automated).

Using Hadoop in the Enterprise

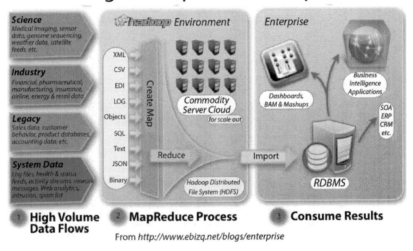

From *http://www.ebizq.net/blogs/enterprise*

Figure 1.3. *The Hadoop MapReduce process*

1.4.3. *And beyond...*

History is yet to be written but Artificial Intelligence is already positioning itself as a strong candidate in this transition. The reconciliation between Big Data and Artificial Intelligence platforms (especially those linked to "Machine Learning") are beginning to make an appearance. Solutions are now available on the market and companies are increasingly interested in them, particularly within the framework of improving customer experience (CXM). In the following chapters, we will discuss how these solutions work and how they could challenge the established order in terms of BI. New BI solutions will (and must) integrate the notion of prescriptive analysis, which goes beyond forecasting (anticipating what will happen and when it will happen) and allows us to understand how and why it will happen based on scenarios of decisions and actions, as well as the associated impacts in order to optimize opportunities and/or minimize or even eliminate risks. Descriptive analysis merely explains a situation based on descriptive variables. It consists of drawing up a "portrait" of the situation as it appears subsequent to compilation and classification of the data based on so-called descriptive variables (which describe the situation we are trying to explain), for example defining customer segments, purchasing behaviors, desire for a product, etc. Descriptive analysis is the data analysis method that is probably the most used by existing BI solutions, whether for sales, marketing, finance or human resources. It answers questions such as "what happened", "when" and "why". This is based on so-called "historical" data (analysis of past data).

2

Digital Learning

In this chapter, we will discuss the two main concepts of digital learning that are linked to Artificial Intelligence: "Deep Learning" or unsupervised deep learning (the system discovers by itself) and "Machine Learning", which is similar to supervised learning (the system learns to discover).

2.1. What is learning?

We could define learning as an iterative process of learning from one's past experiences, or those of others, as training, an explanation, etc., and acting accordingly. The objective of learning is to improve the performance (result) of one's activities (whether manual or intellectual). Subsequently, the question of adaptation (to the natural, commercial, social environment, etc.) is raised. Natural adaptation is an essential characteristic of "life", it is Darwinian and is based on natural selection without learning, where random chance takes precedence. Adaptation to one's social or commercial environment is not a matter of chance, it is an upstream thought, conceived on the basis of information acquired over time through learning (personal experience or through transmission of knowledge).

This approach is the key to humanity's evolution as it allows human beings in the early stages of life to learn fundamental things such as recognizing a voice, a familiar face, learning to understand what is said, to walk and to talk. It allows knowledge to be transferred from generation to generation, which will allow each generation to add their own experiences. The complexity of the world in which we now live has forced us to create a structure for this transfer of knowledge (it now takes twenty years to train an engineer). Our society of information and communication (audiovisual media, Internet) might suggest that learning is equivalent to being informed. This approach is incomplete: information is certainly an important part of the learning cycle, but to inform oneself is not the same as training oneself. For there to be real learning, the learner (the algorithm, in the case of Artificial Intelligence) must be able to choose between several solutions and learn from his or her choices in light of the objective to be achieved (this point will be further discussed in the following sections). This will ultimately translate into experiences (better or worse in terms of objectives) that will gradually form an initial level of learning. It is this level of learning that we find in Artificial Intelligence solutions, called "self-learning".

2.2. Digital learning

The topic of digital learning is not new: decision-making solutions have been able to model past situations for a long time now, often based on very complex statistical processing (for example historical regressions). The aim of this is to identify the structuring elements that are the explanatory variables of the situation we wish to model (for example age, sex, country of origin, socioeconomic profile, purchase history, etc.) in historical data (past transactions). These variables are the keystone of the model. For example, they allow us to explain the purchasing behavior of a customer, the sales rates of a particular product or service, the financial activity of a company, etc. These models will then be used as the "digital memory" of the company and will be one of the inputs (not the only one, but a structuring input) of predictive analysis processes (the ability to predict the future). These analyses are subjected to constant adjustments (given the evolution of probability linked to a prediction in the future; a 24-h weather forecast is often more reliable than a 15-day forecast) such that the management of a company can adapt to the current reality. As long as the modeled elements have exhibited a relatively stable behavior (mostly reproducible over a period of time ranging from a few months to a year), the quality of the forecasts based on this type of modeling is fairly reliable (modulo the probability linked to the standard deviation of the modeled data), with the "static" side of the model being the Achilles heel (the explanatory variables are predefined as the entry point of the model and are difficult to predict). The inertia of models can be added to this, which results in difficulty in adapting to changes (purchasing behavior, customer volatility, various crises, etc.) and can have an impact on business activity.

In some cases, the models cannot adapt (depending on how they were created), which forces new models to be created, models that will take these changes into account. All this translates into a long and complex statistical and data processing task, with the collateral effect of a significant "time to market" (implementation time). In our globalized world that is in constant motion, where time and opportunity are closely linked, it is easy to come up with many situations in which this approach will not be effective enough. It is, however, the basis for many forecasting and optimization solutions.

2.3. The Internet has changed the game

Things got complicated with the advent of a public Internet and thus the birth of e-commerce (from the 1990s), which accelerated exponentially in the 2000s with the "rampant" digitization of our world, with more people being connected to the Internet, and where smartphones and tablets have been vectors for permanent connectivity, anywhere, anytime. Services and content have adapted to new uses. For companies, customer experience is becoming the key word, perceived as the "grail" that will allow companies to gain market share (for those who know how to continuously improve it): the right product at the right price, at the right time, in the right place and for the right customer, whatever the context. And all this in a digitalized world of high behavioral volatility (search engines and product/price comparators are the core of these changes).

This is the challenge that companies are facing, and it is only getting worse. Based on the principle that a decision must be made as closely as possible to its implementation, decision-making systems (customer knowledge databases) have been reconciled with transactional systems (e-commerce Websites, call centers, etc.). This has been made possible because of the implementation of recommendation engines (management of rules). Their function mainly involves associating customer profiles with products/services/content, etc., that could be suitable for them, such as offering a certain number of additional products (upsell) that are related to products in the shopping cart and/or products that have been chosen by Internet users with a similar "profile" (in terms of buying behavior). These recommendation engines are mainly supplied by decision-making systems (as mentioned above) with the main "weaknesses" of a predefinition of the expected result, as models always rely on the same explanatory variables (those used to build the model) at the input of the real-time analysis process. Ultimately, this will result in the same analysis result (for example a customer score) with no or little consideration of the dynamic context of the Internet user (how the user arrived on the Website, what he saw beforehand, has he been to the Website before, etc.). The system's lack of reactivity to a change in behavior (more or less brutal) would require the models to be recalculated (a long and complex analytical process) if those in place happen to become obsolete (and no longer reflect reality). To avoid this, companies set up "consensual" (large spectrum) models that are not very accurate in terms of targeting, but which have the advantage of a certain robustness, although they do not allow or only allow very little personalization (each one is to be treated in a "personal" and differentiated way, and not necessarily as part of a larger entity).

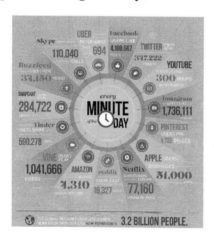

Figure 2.1. *Volume of activity per minute on the Internet (source:*
http://bgr.com/2016/02/03/internet-activity-one-minute/)

The above figure demonstrates the volume of activity per minute on the Internet:

– 347,222 tweets are written;

– 51,000 apps are downloaded from the Apple app store;

– 300 h of videos are posted on YouTube;

– 4,166,667 Facebook users press the "Like" button;

– 694 people order a driver on Uber;

– 110,040 calls are made on Skype;

– 34,150 videos are viewed on BuzzFeed;

– 284,722 Snaps are shared on SnapChat;

– 1,041,666 videos are played on Vine, which did not even exist in 2013;

– 17,336,111 photos are "liked" on Instagram;

– And so on...

2.4. Big Data and the Internet of Things will reshuffle the cards

Things could stay the way they are (and many are at this very stage for the time being) if it were not for Big Data and the Internet of Things ([IoTs] more commonly known as connected devices, some studies [IDC, etc.] predict that there will be over 20 billion [some say 50 billion] devices connected to the Internet by 2020). But what is it all about? The IoT is a set of networks that allows data to be transmitted between physical objects and software agents via an identification system. Connected devices are increasingly present in our daily lives (watches, scales, thermostats, etc.) and this is only the beginning. Very soon, we will also have connected and autonomous cars. Who knows what tomorrow will bring? One thing is certain: we are and will be more and more "connected". Web 2.0 has initiated this movement, creating new needs, generating new opportunities. No one can dispute the influence (societal, political, economic) of social networks in today's society of knowledge and communication. Those who master these modes of communication (and therefore the associated data) will have an advantage over others.

Imagine what the typical day of an entrepreneur could look like in the not too distant future, where most of our everyday objects will be "smart" and connected... In the morning, I am woken up by my "smart bed", which calculated the ideal time (in my sleep cycle) to wake me up. My "smart bed" communicated with my "smart media hub" (Hi-Fi, video, Internet, etc.), which links me up to my favorite web radio station and also to my centralized controller, which controls my bathroom heating and water for a shower. After that, I put on my "smart glasses or lenses", and I am connected to the rest of the world. While I am having breakfast (suggested by my virtual sports coach via my smart glasses), I get a summary of what has happened in the world while I was asleep (I flick from content to content with a simple gesture of my eyes). I take a look at my diary for the day and simultaneously, my "smart fridge" asks me if I would like to place an order for certain products, and suggests some associated products and current promotions, which I validate with the blink of an eye. And then the day truly begins. I get in my smart car (which runs on renewable energy), and I confirm the autopilot to take me to my first meeting. In the meantime, I connect to a videoconference to take stock with my team, and finalize the preparations for this first meeting. I arrive at the location, my car parks itself in a power-charging space (charged by induction), my smart glasses guide me to my meeting (using augmented reality) and announce my imminent arrival to the person I am to meet with. All morning, we work on an urbanization file (I am an architect), with 3D projections of different prototypes, documents are exchanged via the "cloud", even my computer does not serve much purpose – I control all the actions via my "smart glasses" and/or a "smart table" (which serves as Human-Machine Interface). In the meantime, my virtual assistant reminds me that she has to organize a certain number of appointments for the next two days, and asks me to validate them, which I do with a gesture on the "smart table" (though I could also have done it through my smart glasses). The meeting ends, and I video call a friend whom I see is available on the social network to organize a lunch with him. I suggest a restaurant and as we have access to the menu, we choose what we would like to eat while we talk, validate our reservation and the coordinates are sent to my smart car. The smart car takes me to the restaurant, where our table awaits, and the first dish is served within a few minutes of our arrival. The afternoon will be spent working on a joint project (in connected mode) with my collaborators (who are spread across multiple continents) and on the urbanization file for which we will validate a prototype so that we can materialize it on our 3D printer in order to present it the next day. The work day ends, I read over some messages that were pending, including an invitation (from my local sports club) to play an hour of tennis tonight (with a player I have never met but who has a similar level to me), which I accept. I then go to the tennis club via home, and my smart car chooses the optimal route. In the meantime, a drone has delivered my new racket that I ordered the day before. At the beginning of the evening, I arrive home for dinner with my family (it is now 8:30 pm), then I watch a sporting event (with a few connected friends, where everyone can see and review the action through their own smart glasses and from any angle they wish by connecting to one of the 50 cameras that broadcast the event). It is 11 pm and I receive a message from my smart bed suggesting a sleep duration of 6 h (having taken the next day's agenda into account). I decide to follow this advice and disconnect from the virtual world to enter a dream world....

In order for this (presumably quite near) future to be possible, connected devices will need to be given full autonomy. This autonomy has a name: Artificial Intelligence. These are new algorithms that will allow connected devices to acquire the skills needed to solve problems or perform tasks. These technologies have opened up new horizons in terms of knowledge and customer care (the traces we leave [voluntarily or not] on the Internet say a lot about us). This allows better customer knowledge – we could speak of "augmented customers" (each new visit will enrich this informational heritage). It also allows new health services to be set up (the connected patient), as well as transport (the connected and autonomous car), home automation (smart home) and so on.... To be able to take advantage of this manna, this new Eldorado, these enormous volumes of information (Big Data) must be able to be processed in order to draw the right lessons from it – and all this must be done in real time (which is where Artificial Intelligence comes into play). We will be shifting from a digitalized world to a connected world, where most of the elements that surround us, which we wear and use, will be connected and will produce data 24 h a day (see Figure 2.2). Today, companies are taking the IoTs into serious consideration in their strategies for improving customer experience.

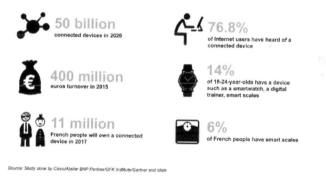

Source: Study done by Cisco/Atelier BNP Paribas/GFK Institute/Gartner and Idate

Figure 2.2. *Some key figures concerning connected devices*

2.5. Artificial Intelligence linked to Big Data will undoubtedly be the keystone of digital learning

Today, only sophisticated algorithms are capable of processing Big Data in real time. In recent years, this raw material that is Big Data has allowed the comeback of Artificial Intelligence, which will learn ever more quickly with increasing amounts of data to "consume" (and the Internet is a source of data that seems to be inexhaustible). Big Data processing solutions can aggregate, summarize and expose large volumes of data from heterogeneous sources, and Artificial Intelligence will make it possible to extract all the value from them. Artificial Intelligence will be used in addition to Big Data to extract meaning, determine better results based on continuous learning and enable real-time decision making.

The convergence of Big Data and Artificial Intelligence technologies will accompany the digital transformation of our world and must be seen as an opportunity with an analytical potential that is capable of changing a company and its strategy. Artificial Intelligence turns out to be a really gifted "pupil". But how can we ensure that a computer program learns from its experience? In other words, what we are asking is: could this be possible without the intervention of a programmer who would modify its operation, through the mere assessment of a result for each of its tasks relative to the objectives assigned? Is a computer program capable, like a child, of learning from its environment? While there is still a long way to go, machine learning (supervised or unsupervised) has made significant progress in recent years, driven in particular by large companies that have made massive investments in this field. One of the most publicized technical feats was undoubtedly the Google Brain, which in 2012 allowed a machine to discover the concept of chat by analyzing millions of (unlabeled) images from the web.

2.6. Supervised learning

The most common machine learning technique is supervised learning: the aim of it is to specialize the machine in recognition of one or other element, which would be contained in a digital data stream (image, sound, etc.). This technique implies that we have an idea of the expected result, for example recognizing a car in an image. In order for a program to learn to recognize an object, a face, a sound or something else, we must submit tens of thousands (or even millions) of images annotated as such. This training may require days of processing, and will be supervised by analysts to check that learning takes place, or even to correct errors (which would not be considered by the program). After this training stage, new images (that have never been used in the learning phase) are proposed to the program, with the objective of evaluating the level of learning of the machine (in other words, discovering the elements that were part of the learning in the new images). This technique is relatively old, but it has taken a leap forward with recent technological advances. The masses of data now available and the computational power available to engineers have multiplied the efficiency of algorithms. This new generation of supervised learning is already part of our everyday life: machine translation tools are the perfect example. By analyzing huge databases that combine texts and their translation, the program finds statistical regularities on which it bases itself for the most probable translation not only of a word, but also of a phrase or even a sentence.

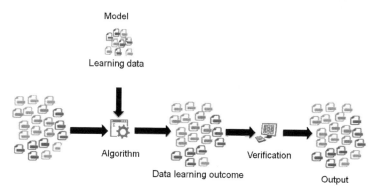

Figure 2.3. *Supervised learning*

Supervised learning has four stages:

1) we have an idea of what the output should be;

2) we teach the machine to recognize images with labeled data (learning data, which will be used as a model);

3) raw data (to be classified) is inserted into the machine;

4) we verify the result, then produce the output.

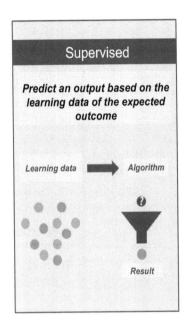

Figure 2.4. *Supervised learning*

2.7. Enhanced supervised learning

The enhancement of supervised learning is based on a "reward" mode that is linked to learning the correlation between the inputs (models that will be used for the task at hand) and the output (the expected result). The "reward" is in fact an estimation of the error (the ratio between failure and success), which will be propagated (in the form of weights/probability) in each of the models used for the task. Through this process, the system knows whether or not the output it provides is correct, but it does not know the correct answer.

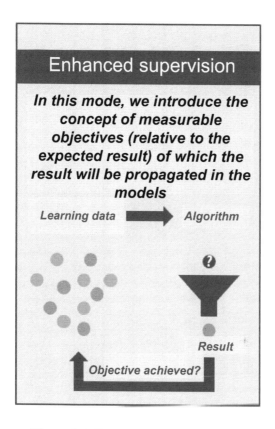

Figure 2.5. *Enhanced supervised learning*

Enhanced supervised learning involves setting up a principle to measure the result relative to the objectives to be achieved. This measurement (positive or negative) will be propagated in the models, and will have the function of refining the probability of a particular model in its contribution to the task.

Let us consider a use case: a purchase on the Internet via an e-commerce website, with the objective that the customer places an order. We take the profile of the customer, which will be formally determined if the customer is registered, or informally if he is navigating anonymously (in this case, we will have less information to allow "targeting").

1) A client profile is composed of variables such as age, sex, place of residence, household members, socio-economic level, etc. (there are hundreds of variables).

2) These variables are organized in bins, which group together all the customer profiles.

For example, the age bin contains the age distribution of all customers by age groups (in our case, the age of the customer is 32 years old, which corresponds to entry 4 of the age bin between 30 and 33 years old).

Bin : Age	1	2	3	4	5	6	7	8	9	10	11	12
				x							·	
	20	25	30	33	37	42	46	50	54	59	65 (age)	

3) Every piece of customer information will allow us to find its input in the corresponding bin.

For example, bin var2 could be the number of household members (and in this case, 2 would be equal to single). We apply the same principle for all variables of the client's profile (NB: these elements are statistically defined by analysts when setting up the system).

	age	var 2	var 3	var 4	var 5	var 6	var 7	var 8	var 9	var 10 ...
bin	4	6	4	11	9	4	8	2	2	6

4) We then use these elements to index the table containing the weights/probability of each of the variables of this client's profile.

bin	age	var 2	var 3	var 4	var 5	var 6	var 7	var 8 .	var 9	var 10 ...
	4	6	4	11	9	4	8	2	2	6

	age	var 2	var 3	var 4	var 5	var 6	var 7	var 8	var 9	var 10
bin 1	-0.018	0.035	0.012	-0.003	0.043	0.044	0.007	-0.017	-0.026	0.010
bin 2	0.931	-0.012	-0.035	0.002	-0.035	0.029	0.022	-0.014	0.035	0.011
bin 3	0.193	0.009	-0.012	0.037	-0.025	0.044	-0.041	-0.003	0.000	-0.030
bin 4	0.116	-0.029	0.034	-0.018	0.026	-0.016	0.050	-0.036	0.033	-0.048
bin 5	0.940	-0.015	0.007	-0.032	0.020	0.017	-0.031	0.026	-0.043	0.043
bin 6	0.234	0.029	0.024	0.011	-0.046	0.013	0.044	0.019	-0.023	-0.010
bin 7	0.770	0.029	-0.049	-0.035	-0.049	0.032	-0.010	-0.008	-0.025	0.048
bin 8	0.480	0.023	0.000	0.047	-0.012	0.021	0.027	-0.038	0.033	-0.026
bin 9	0.989	0.005	-0.036	0.018	0.013	0.004	-0.041	-0.021	0.023	0.022
bin 10	0.448	-0.036	-0.035	0.036	-0.028	-0.050	-0.014	0.043	0.045	0.030
bin 11	0.425	-0.031	0.027	0.002	-0.018	-0.014	0.050	0.024	-0.019	-0.027
bin 12	0.653	-0.023	0.038	-0.039	0.047	0.021	-0.028	0.037	-0.002	0.016

We then add up the probabilities: 0.116 + 0.029 + 0.034 + 0.002 + 0.013 + 0.016 + 0.027 + 0.014 + 0.035 + 0.010 = 0.217, which corresponds to the probability (21.7 %) that the task achieves the objective (as a reminder, the objective is that an order is placed).

5) Evaluation of the result of the action (the "reward").

– Probability of the order being placed: 0.217.

– The order is placed: 1.

– Error estimate: 1 – 0.217 = 0.783 (the prediction in this case was too low, at 78%).

– We use this value, which will be weighted (in our case by multiplying by 0.01 as this weighting factor is calculated relative to the global contribution of this action to the model. In short, the more actions we have (for example, number of visits per day to the e-commerce website), the lower this factor is). This gives: $0.783 \times 0.01 = 0.00783$.

– We then add this value, 0.00783 (the "reward"), to each bin used for this action (yellow box here below, which will give bin 4 of the age variable: $0.116 + 0.00783 = 0.123$. This will have the effect of quickly aligning the models to reality (which can change very quickly!)

bin	age	var 2	var 3	var 4	var 5	var 6	var 7	var 8	. var 9	var 10 ...
	4	6	4	11	9	4	8	2	2	6

	age	var 2	var 3	var 4	var 5	var 6	var 7	var 8	var 9	var 10
bin 1	-0.018	0.035	0.012	-0.003	0.043	0.044	0.007	-0.017	-0.026	0.010
bin 2	0.931	-0.012	-0.035	-0.002	-0.035	0.029	0.022	-0.014	0.035	-0.011
bin 3	0.193	0.009	-0.012	0.037	-0.025	0.044	-0.041	-0.003	0.000	-0.030
bin 4	0.116	-0.029	0.034	-0.018	0.026	-0.016	0.050	-0.036	0.033	-0.043
bin 5	0.940	-0.015	0.007	-0.032	0.020	0.017	-0.031	0.026	-0.043	0.048
bin 6	0.234	0.029	0.024	0.011	-0.046	0.013	0.044	0.019	-0.023	-0.010
bin 7	0.770	0.029	-0.049	-0.035	-0.049	0.032	-0.010	-0.008	-0.025	0.048
bin 8	0.480	0.023	0.000	0.047	-0.012	0.021	0.027	-0.038	0.033	-0.026
bin 9	0.989	0.005	-0.036	0.018	0.013	0.004	-0.041	-0.021	0.023	0.022
bin 10	0.448	-0.036	-0.035	0.036	-0.028	-0.050	-0.014	0.043	0.045	0.030
bin 11	0.425	-0.031	0.027	0.002	-0.018	-0.014	0.050	0.024	-0.019	-0.027
bin 12	0.653	-0.023	0.038	-0.039	0.047	0.021	-0.028	0.037	-0.002	0.016

2.8. Unsupervised learning

Unsupervised learning holds perhaps the greatest promise for Artificial Intelligence. This is the type of learning we find in nature. Knowledge is built on a combination of knowledge and experience. These experiences will be the driving force behind our learning. Unsupervised learning is what allows humans and animals to understand how to evolve in their environment, adapt to it and ultimately survive. Unlike supervised learning, the algorithm has no information about the data it needs to process, we could say that it is "agnostic" or "self-taught". It proceeds by grouping together (clustering) and gathering similar information. This is a very effective technique when you have no (or little) idea of what is contained in the information (contrary to supervised learning, where you have an idea of the expected result), which can reveal something that would not naturally come to mind (using the "hidden" side of the data).

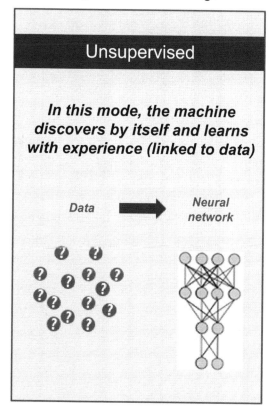

Figure 2.6. *Unsupervised learning*

Unsupervised learning is a mode of learning that could be called "self-taught". The machine learns by itself through a method known as "clustering" (grouping of identical elements).

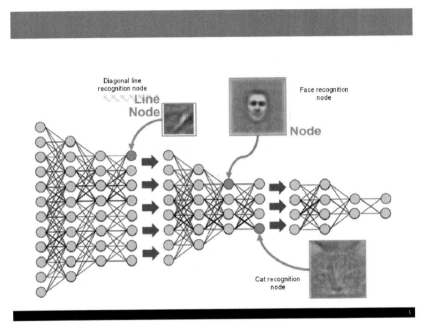

Figure 2.7. *Neural networks*

Neural networks are organized in successive layers and will allow step-by-step identification (layer of increasingly complex treatments) of objects, faces, animals, etc.

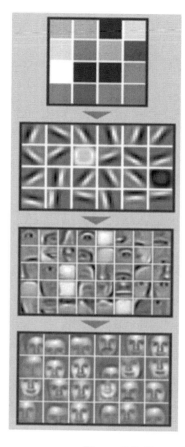

Layer 1: the machine detects the light and dark pixels

Layer 2: the machine learns to identify simple shapes

Layer 3: the machine learns to identify complex shapes

Layer 4: the machine learns to identify which shapes can be used to define a human face

Figure 2.8. *Example of facial recognition*

3

The Reign of Algorithms

A new form of intelligence is emerging before us. It does not come from the living being but is created by mankind in the form of algorithms that are capable of solving problems and performing tasks. This new form of intelligence is different from our own: it perceives the world through the prism of Big Data, it has its own logic, it seems to be from elsewhere and this elsewhere is the major development centers of key digital players: IBM, Google, Microsoft, Facebook, Uber... Not a week goes by without there being some new announcement in this field, where we learn that an Artificial Intelligence (AI) solution has just surpassed our own intelligence in areas as varied as strategy games (in 2017, Alphago beat the best Go player in the world, Ke Jie), facial recognition, various diagnoses (medical, etc.), autonomous transport (in 2016, Uber proposed an autonomous car service)... It would seem that no sector has been left out. These algorithms are based on neural networks modeled from the functioning of our own brain neurons (see Figure 3.1). These algorithms are capable of learning (just like humans) and ultimately discovering the world around them by themselves. This new form of intelligence is completely original, it does not start from anything *a priori* (no cultural or societal "pre-coding"). It is more than just a technological evolution – we speak of a revolution, one which we are not yet measuring the impact of on our digital society.

3.1. What is an algorithm?

The word "algorithm" comes from the name of the great ninth-Century Persian mathematician Al Khwarizmi (Latinized to *Algoritmi*) and the title of one of his works (The Compendious Book on Calculation by Completion and Balancing) originated the word algebra. It was him who disseminated the decimal number in the West (brought back from India). According to John MacCormick, a computer scientist from Oxford University and author of "Nine Algorithms that Changed the Future", an algorithm is no more than a "precise recipe that specifies the exact sequence of steps required to solve a problem" (the simplest example of this is probably a cooking recipe). This then raises the question of a computer algorithm, which can be used to classify, select, join, predict... These algorithms are a set of instructions in the form of lines of code (programs), which use data (Data or even Big Data) as ingredients for their "recipe". Behind these algorithms are many engineers, computer scientists and mathematicians who are responsible for programming them (to date, an algorithm has always been thought of by a human being first). What makes these algorithms efficient is the data they manipulate and for some, the results that they remember (linked to the objective to be reached), which will render them self-learning thus creating a new form of intelligence. We call this "Artificial Intelligence (AI)". We can therefore conclude that this form of intelligence is mainly driven by data.

3.2. A brief history of AI

It is a chaotic story, with many twists and turns, always on the brink of hope and disappointment, and embellished in its entirety by a strong capillarity with technology: the computing capacity of computers, as well as the availability of data (Big Data). But it also concerns the "problems" to be solved, the "digitization" of our world, which has accelerated exponentially since the beginning of the 21st century and has opened up new horizons for AI: transport (the autonomous and connected car), smart homes (the connected house), health (the connected patient) and customer experience (customization) are just some of the fields at the forefront of this topic.

3.2.1. Between the 1940s and 1950s

The first steps of AI. This period is considered as the beginning of AI, with the creation of the first neural networks. The work of two neurologists, Warren McCulloch and Walter Pitts in 1943 ("A Logical Calculus of the Ideas Immanent in Nervous Activity"), led to the first mathematical model of the biological neuron, the artificial neuron (see Figure 3.1). It was in fact a binary neuron, of which the output could only be 0 or 1. To calculate this output, the neuron calculated a weighted sum of its inputs (which, like the outputs of other artificial neurons, also equaled 0 or 1) and then applied a threshold activation function: if the weighted sum exceeded a certain value, the output of the neuron was 1, otherwise it was equal to 0.

An artificial neuron generally has several inputs and one output that corresponds, respectively, to the dendrites and the emergence cone of the biological neuron (the starting point of the axon). The excitatory and inhibitory actions of synapses are represented by weight coefficients (weights) associated with each input. These weighting coefficients (for each input) are updated (upwards for excitation or downwards for inhibition), with each activation of the neuron depending on the result related to the objective of this activation. Ultimately, this leads to a form of learning.

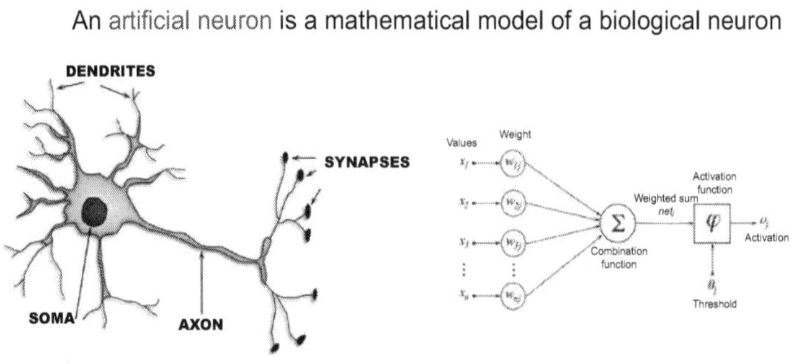

An artificial neuron is a mathematical model of a biological neuron

Figure 3.1. *The artificial neuron and the mathematical model of a biological neuron*

In 1956, the term AI was finally adopted after a Dartmouth conference led by computer scientists. The conference was on the theme of intelligence and the idea of an "intelligent" machine:

– How to simulate thought and language through formal rules?

– How to make a neural network think?

– How to equip a machine with automatic learning capacity?

– How to equip a machine with creativity?

3.2.2. *Beginning of the 1960s*

This was a very promising period, with a lot of buzz around AI. A large number of programs were developed to solve diverse and varied problems, such as:

– proving mathematical theorems;

– playing checkers;

– solving puzzles;

– first attempts at machine translation;

– and more...

3.2.3. *The 1970s*

A return to reality, the beginning of disappointment. The lack of results (taking into account promises made in the previous decade) and the difficulty of implementation due to a lack of computing power (for computers at the time) considerably slowed down the progress of existing AI programs. In addition, in their book "Perceptrons" (1969), Minsky and Papert demonstrated that neural networks at the time could not calculate some very simple functions (like distinguishing two numbers written in binary), which led to a "crisis" in this branch of AI with the entirety of automatic learning being called into question.

3.2.4. *The 1980s*

AIs return to grace with the development of the first expert systems. An expert system is an "intelligent computer program that uses knowledge and inference procedures to solve problems that were difficult enough to require significant human expertise for their solutions" [FEI 82]. For example:

With 450 rules, MYCIN (an expert system used for the diagnosis of blood infections) was able to diagnose infections to a level close to that of human experts.

The computer manufacturer DEC (Digital Equipment) set up an expert system to help configure its computers (which saved millions of dollars).

3.2.5. *The 1990s*

A lot of work on neural networks, with the "rediscovery" (the initial discovery was at the end of the 1960s, but without much ado at the time) of the "back-propagation" learning rule ("errors" between the desired outputs and the observed outputs, and retro-propagation, from the output to the inputs, with the effect of adapting W (weight) neuron by neuron).

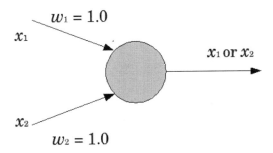

Figure 3.2. *X1 and X2 are the input data, W1 and W2 are the relative weights (which will be used as weighting) for the confidence (performance) of these inputs, allowing the output to choose between the X1 or X2 data. It is very clear that W (the weight) will be the determining element of the decision. Being able to adapt it in retro-propagation will make the system self-learning*

3.2.6. *The 2000s*

AI gained ground, and it "infiltrated" companies (some of the biggest being Google, Amazon, Netflix, etc.) based on two important developments:

1) The use of the Graphic Processing Unit (GPU) instead of the Central Processing Unit, which we find in computers.

The GPU was originally designed for matrix array image processing (less computing power, but more parallelization) and allows parallel processing. As each GPU represents a neuron, there are platforms that contain hundreds or even thousands of GPUs, which encompass just as many neurons. For example, IBM's TrueNorth chip contains 5.4 billion transistors and creates 1 million neurons and 256 million synapses.

2) The continuous digitization of our world around the Internet and connected devices (which are only at the beginning of their story) is the source of "Big Data". These Big Data have become (as never seen before) the raw material necessary to feed these algorithms.

The combination of these two developments act as a catalyst for AI, which is gradually occupying fields as varied as: gaming, medicine, transport, home automation, personal assistants... And we are only at the beginning of this chapter in history.

3.3. Algorithms are based on neural networks, but what does this mean?

Over the past decade, we have seen significant development in AI solutions based on neural networks. This trend started with the implementation of AI solutions in fields as varied as: medicine, transport, finance, commerce, facial recognition, sound, images... In the world of statistical analysis, neural networks are taking up more and more space, the main reasons being their ability to handle very complex situations (correlation of hundreds or even thousands of variables, etc.) and their ability to adapt (in a world that gets more digital every day) and their (relative) ease of use. "Deep neural network architectures" have become key words in terms of AI solutions, inspired by the organization of the human brain.

A network of deep neurons is simply a computer program made up of tens of thousands of interconnected mathematical functions, like neurons and their synapses.

These neurons are organized in successive layers (the largest networks have over 100 layers). Each neuron processes information from the upper layer and propagates the result to the lower layer (the next one). The level of processed information becomes increasingly complex as the information spreads to the lower layers (See Figure 3.3).

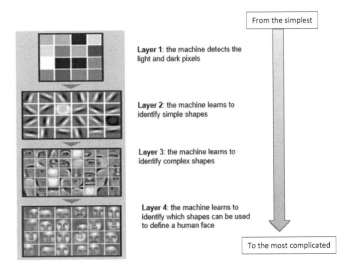

Figure 3.3. *Example of facial recognition*

Neural networks are organized in successive layers and will allow step-by-step (layer of increasingly complex treatments) identification of objects, faces, animals, etc.

The ability to learn from examples is one of the many features of neural networks that allows users to model their data and establish precise rules that will guide the underlying relationships between different data attributes. This technique is called classification (or discrimination); classifying a set of elements means assigning each of these elements a class (or category) among several classes (defined in advance, or not, depending on whether it is in supervised or unsupervised learning mode). Statisticians use the term "classification" for this task, and the algorithm that performs this task is the classifier. Classification is not necessarily used to produce a binary answer (belonging or not belonging to a class) but can provide information on the probability of belonging to a class, which ultimately makes it possible to link the classifiers between each other (where each will have its probability of belonging).

Once this information is established, much more complex classification tasks can be carried out. Neural network users collect representative data and then call upon learning algorithms (supervised or unsupervised), that automatically learn the structure of the data (classification). One of the strengths of this technique is that the user does not need any particular heuristic knowledge on how to select and prepare the data (in relation to the expected result) on the right neural network to choose. The level of knowledge that the user needs to successfully apply neural networks is significantly lower than that required for most traditional data analysis techniques and tools.

Neural networks allow us to break new ground in terms of data analysis; they know how to reveal the hidden side of data, give them meaning and extract rules and trends. Given these characteristics and their extended field of application, neural networks are particularly well-suited to concrete problems in scientific, commercial and industrial research.

Below are a number of areas in which neural networks have already successfully been applied:

- signal processing (network analysis);

- process management;

- robotics;

- classification;

- data preprocessing;

– recognition of shapes;

– image analysis and speech synthesis;

– diagnosis and medical monitoring;

– stock market and forecasts;

– request for loans or real estate loans.

3.4. Why do Big Data and AI work so well together?

"Traditional" Business Intelligence solutions (those that have been in place since the early 2000s) have great difficulty integrating Big Data, which continues to exponentially fill our digital world every day. This situation has resulted in many companies transforming Big Data into "Dark Data" (poorly or not visible data, which are ignored in analytical processes and which are loosely spoken about but never really see the light of day). The main reasons for this are:

– a lack of structured data (images, sounds, blogs, text, etc.), which makes it difficult to integrate them into existing Business Intelligence solutions (highly structured relational databases[1] (operational reporting) or OLAP[2] (multidimensional analyses)). This aspect of the problem was

---

1 Wikipedia: A relational database is a digital database based on the relational model of data, as proposed by E. F. Codd in 1970. A software system used to maintain relational databases is a relational database management system (RDBMS). Virtually all relational database systems use SQL (Structured Query Language) for querying and maintaining the database. This model organizes data into one or more tables (or "relations") of columns and rows, with a unique key identifying each row. Rows are also called records or tuples. Columns are also called attributes. Generally, each table/relation represents one "entity type" (such as customer or product). The rows represent instances of that type of entity (such as "Lee" or "chair") and the columns representing values attributed to that instance (such as address or price).

2 OLAP: Online Analytical Processing is a term used for databases dedicated to data analysis (where often very large volumes of data are stored). They have a special structure (star-shaped model) that allows easy access.

solved with the advent of Hadoop solutions (around 2010, driven by major digital players like Google), which specialized in Big Data processing.

– "Traditional" analytical processes, which have been clogged by the large amount (volume and variety) of variables to be correlated (see Figure 3.4).

– The temporality of analysis, decision and action. "Traditional" Business Intelligence solutions are not/not very well connected to the transactional world (except through certain "emissaries" that are recommendation engines). This induces a lack of responsiveness and adaptation to change. The constraints imposed by "traditional" Business Intelligence solutions do not or barely allow us to exploit this new EL Dorado of Big Data. AI will make it possible to shift the lines to implement processes for decision-making, automated and self-learning actions, in a time frame of just a few milliseconds. An increase in the number of connected devices supported by the digitization of our world will only increase the volume of information available (every second, we produce 6,000 tweets, 40,000 Google searches and 2 million e-mails). By 2019, the volume of available data will exceed 2 zettabytes[3] per year. It would seem that only the convergence between Big Data and AI will make it possible to extract all the value from this information. Large companies are making no mistake; they have already begun this convergence.

---

3 Zettabyte: 10^{21} bytes = 1000000000000000000000 bytes.

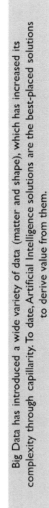

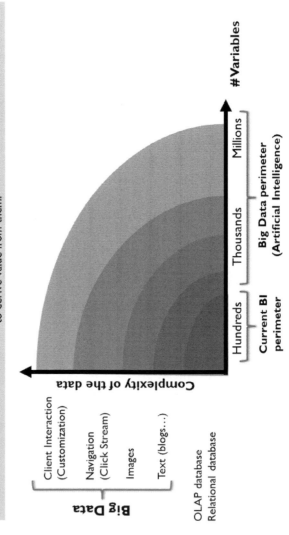

Big Data = Greater variety of data

Big Data has introduced a wide variety of data (matter and shape), which has increased its complexity through capillarity. To date, Artificial Intelligence solutions are the best-placed solutions to derive value from them.

Figure 3.4. *Big Data and variety of data*

Relational or OLAP databases (for analysis) usually impose a data structure that prohibits (or at least complicates) the integration and therefore downstream exploitation (analysis) of the unstructured data that is Big Data. The storage and processing solutions of Big Data (Hadoop...) are backed by AI solutions that have solved this problem.

4

Uses for Artificial Intelligence

The Artificial Intelligence market is currently booming, with the majority of large companies investing hugely in R&D in the field. Google, Apple, Facebook and Amazon (GAFA) have allocated several thousand engineers to it, as well as several billion dollars, but so have states (France invested 1.5 billion euro in 2015, *"France IA"*).

With the digitization of our world, where none are spared (companies are being digitized more and more with each passing day), nearly all industries are in some way affected by the expansion of Artificial Intelligence. This will gradually change relations between the different internal actors (employees) and external actors (customers, suppliers).

This chapter will focus on the uses for Artificial Intelligence, though this will be far from exhaustive. Uses will include:

– customer relations: personalization becomes key;

– transport: cars and other autonomous forms of transportation;

– medicine: help with diagnosis;

– home automation: the smart home;

– intelligent agents or personal assistants: worthy heirs to our smartphones;

– image, sound and facial recognition;

– recommendation tools;

– and by definition, all possible uses arising from learning (supervised or not) that would be transmitted to algorithms (via Big Data – who knows what tomorrow will bring...).

In this chapter, we will discuss some of these uses.

4.1. Customer experience management

Customer relationship management (CRM) underwent some major development at the end of the 20th Century with the advent of the Internet and e-commerce websites. More than an evolution, it was a revolution for the consumer, who could now compare multiple offers of goods or services in just a few clicks. These new opportunities had a direct impact on the relationships between suppliers (mainly but not limited to brands) and their customers, who ultimately became "everyone's" customers. This is where companies became aware that what they thought they were "their customers" no longer "belonged" to them; the time a customer spent visiting their e-commerce website or contacting their call center was the only thing that could be used in the context of a customer relationship. This awareness led to CRM. These systems involved building customer knowledge databases, which were mainly based on data from transactional sales systems (such as e-commerce websites or call centers), with the basic premise that the customer is known/recognized in one way or another (which is difficult when the customer navigates "anonymously" without an official registration to a website). Riding on the wave of technological development of communication tools (smartphones, tablets), social media networks arrived into a world that is becoming more digitalized every day, where Internet connection is permanent. We could even say that the source of these changes is major changes in customer relations. On social networks, it is the customers who have "control": they decide when and how they want to interact with a company. Through their collaborative way of working, social media networks promote the exchange and sharing of information on social subjects, but also relating to a brand, a product and more... an experience (there you have it, we have finally said the word!). It is much simpler and more efficient to share content (images, videos, etc.) and give your opinion on social media networks such as Facebook in the context of sharing with your community, or just to leave a comment somewhere, than to answer satisfaction surveys (by post or phone, or even on the Internet). This new approach to customer relations led to the birth of social CRM. For the first time ever, companies had to take the social dimension of their customer relations into account, which has forced them to rethink their point of contact strategy. Social CRM has developed the communication between a company and its customers; the customer used to be downstream of this communication flow, targeted among so many others (identified as being in a same segment, in other words with another user who has shown a more or less identical purchasing behavior) in one or other marketing campaign. Toward more interactive modes of communication, the customer and his provider are now in direct or indirect contact via social media networks. This allows several things: first and foremost, to build a more humane, more natural, more direct relationship with customers, and even to make them contribute to the creation of goods or services that would best suit them. But above all, it increases the knowledge that companies have of their customers through their integration in marketing databases for the interactions on different social media networks such as Facebook, Twitter, forums, etc. Social CRM makes it possible to considerably enrich the CRM by supplying data that are very difficult or impossible to obtain through classic customer relations channels. For example, with social CRM not only can you track what your customers think of your company, but also what your customers are saying about your company to their networks. Social networks are by far the best place to find out what is being said about you. Social CRM allows you to expand the scope of CRM and take a big step toward customer experience management (CXM) through a more refined and expanded understanding of your customers. Social CRM is a component of CXM; it goes beyond simple interactions between the customer and a company, and it extends it to its individual network.

4.1.1. *What role have smartphones and tablets played in this relationship?*

Today, it is impossible to talk about customer relations without mentioning the devices that allow us to connect to our digital world anywhere and at any time. These mobile devices (which never leave our sides) have profoundly modified the interactions between a company and its customers. Mobile devices (smartphone or tablet, from the moment we have them and they are connected to the Internet) are now used to search for a trip, to compare products between websites, to contact customer service, to file notices, to process administrative activities, and much more. Recent studies have shown a rise in the power of mobile in terms of customer experience. Here are some examples to highlight this:

– over half of the French population owns a smartphone;

– at least one-third owns a tablet;

– mobile apps are the main digital tool for optimizing the mobile customer experience;

– over half of all businesses (active in the digital customer relations world) want to quickly improve their mobile customer experience;

– mobile devices can be used to optimize customer proximity.

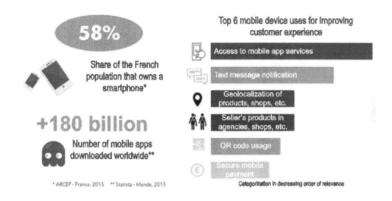

Figure 4.1. *Markess 2016 public study*

4.1.2. *CXM is more than just a software package*

CXM is not just about implementing a CXM application. CXM is a new approach to customer relations, an approach that aims to align the whole company, and not just the few services (marketing or sales) that were the only ones to manage this relationship in practice. We are referring to a paradigm shift for companies, where each point of contact (regardless of what the company does) contributes to the experience; we are talking about being "customer centric". CXM mainly surpasses CRM through its will to dive deeper into knowledge about the customer journey, by capturing interactions (of all types, whether online, offline, consumption, etc.), with the aim of improving and optimizing the customer experience by personalizing and individualizing this experience. This approach, which involves all levels within a company, is really at the heart of the CXM philosophy. CXM is clearly part of the CRM evolution, which involves mastering and controlling the points of contact between a company and its customers. Mastering this implies integrating different solutions (computer applications) to manage these contact points, as well as exhaustively capturing the data relating to these points of contact (Big Data). This Big Data will then be the raw material for analyzing and controlling processes in this experience, and, for the most advanced companies in this field, will feed Artificial Intelligence solutions that will extract value from this information (see Figure 4.2).

The principle of CXM is that companies "individualize" the requirements of their customers by providing them with a constantly renewed, personalized, interactive and targeted experience at every stage of their journey. CXM must integrate customization tools to recommend the best products and guide the conversion through automated cross-channel and customization solutions. The CXM approach aims to offer a service, an individual experience, by placing customer expectations at the heart of the company's responsibilities (centering the company's processes on the customer). It is therefore imperative to involve teams across the entire company and not just those dedicated to customer relations. Every employee in the company must be convinced of his or her contribution to this experience.

4.1.3. *Components of CXM*

Figure 4.2. *What is CXM?*

4.1.3.1. *Client interactions*

This is the integration layer in the information system that will allow real-time exchange of information between the customer and his or her various information sources. In our increasingly digital and connected world, where time and mobility are key, customers want to access the desired information quickly and from anywhere. This includes the price and availability of a product, reserving activities (trips, tickets, etc.), personal data, administrative services and social networks. The Internet is positioned as the most appropriate medium to meet these expectations (which have in fact become needs).

4.1.3.2. *Web content management*

This mainly involves customizing the content to be in line with the customer's profile and aligned with the company's contact policy. But it also means being able to adapt to the user's journey (sales dialog), for example by presenting transport options sooner, once the customer is identified as being from another country or even depending on the stage at which he is in his journey and/or according to the contents in his shopping cart.

4.1.3.3. *E-commerce and web apps*

E-commerce websites and mobile applications must be designed to allow customization (see point above). This requires a formal division between the presentation layer (mechanisms that allow content to be presented, but also the navigation sequence) and the interaction management layer (data exchanges and/or business rules). Without this division, it is likely that dynamic customization of content and/or browsing will be difficult or even impossible.

4.1.3.4. *Big Data, Data Lake, Data Management Platform*

Data (contact data, purchasing data, etc.) are the raw material of CXM (which acts as a customer reference system). It can be of different formats and different sizes (see Chapter 2). CXM relies on these data (via analytical and/or Artificial Intelligence processes) to interact with the customer.

Some common solutions are as follows:

– Big Data architectures using Hadoop technologies (all data formats are possible: logs, e-mails, images, sounds, blogs, etc.);

– Data Lakes, which are databases (like Big Data) where data are structured at the time of its reading;

– Data Management Platform, which is an integrated version of the two points above.

4.1.3.5. *Recommendations and/or Artificial Intelligence*

This is the keystone of CXM, where optimization of the customer experience will be played out, being the analytical dimension of this architecture. It often combines data analysis algorithms (via data mining analytical processes or self-learning Artificial Intelligence solutions) and a recommendation engine, which is in charge of optimizing the customer experience (under the control of an analytical brick).

4.2. The transport industry

For several years now, manufacturers have been increasing their ingenuity in integrating new technologies into passenger vehicles and public transport in order to make everyday life easier. Thanks to increasingly sophisticated techniques, transportation vehicles such as cars, planes, trains, etc., are now more reliable and more efficient.

Today, we already have a lot of technology in our cars. They are connected, equipped with different sensors, radars, cameras, GPS, cruise control... The autonomous car is only a continuation of progress that has already been made in the last two decades in this field, with the ultimate goal of not needing a driver at all. The main purposes of this approach are as follows:

– to improve road safety;

– improve traffic flow;

– rethink the car's usage model;

– optimize the time spent while in transportation, using this time for something other than driving.

Road safety is the foremost reason, since it is estimated that over 80% of road accidents are caused by human error. If all cars were autonomous and connected, the number of road accidents would fall dramatically: cars would react more quickly and, above all, more rationally in the event of danger. There would be no more speeding and unpredictable behavior (aside from during the transition period, between cars that are already autonomous and those that are not).

If the entire fleet of vehicles was replaced with self-driving cars, traffic in cities would be much more fluid. There would be almost no more traffic jams because the whole network would be interconnected and cars would no longer be parked, as they would be able to park themselves in the nearest parking lot after dropping you off. The usage model of a private car will undoubtedly see an impact: it will no longer be necessary to learn to drive and there would no longer be any limitation on usage (age, health, vision, etc.). It is very likely that this will have an impact on the current model of public transport, so there would be no real reason to own a car at all. We will be able to optimize transport time by making it more useful (like having a video conference from your car, for example).

It seems clear that this chapter of history has already begun, and nothing seems to be able to stop it. In the next decade, we will witness a revolution in mass and individual transport. However, certain legal and ethical aspects of concepts will need to be clarified:

– responsibility in the event of an accident. In theory, the driver would no longer be directly responsible for an accident;

– how should the autonomous car (and hence the algorithms that control it) react in a situation where people (such as a child suddenly crossing the street without warning) could be involved in an accident?

– the technological risk associated with "hacking" [1], where ill-intentioned people could remotely take control of vehicles.

So far, five States in the United States have already authorized autonomous vehicles. France, for its part, has so far only authorized test areas under the Energy Transition Act.

THE AUTONOMOUS CAR

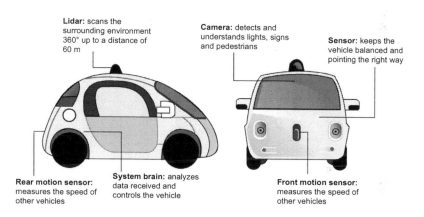

Lidar: scans the surrounding environment 360° up to a distance of 60 m

Camera: detects and understands lights, signs and pedestrians

Sensor: keeps the vehicle balanced and pointing the right way

Rear motion sensor: measures the speed of other vehicles

System brain: analyzes data received and controls the vehicle

Front motion sensor: measures the speed of other vehicles

Figure 4.3. *How does the autonomous car work?*

First, there is a detector: the lidar. This is a laser remote sensing system that scans the direct environment of the car (360° up to 60 meters) and produces a detailed three-

---

1 From Wikipedia: "A security hacker is someone who seeks to breach defenses and exploit weaknesses in a computer system or network. Hackers may be motivated by a multitude of reasons, such as profit, protest, information gathering, challenge, recreation or to evaluate system weaknesses to assist in formulating defenses against potential hackers".

dimensional map of the surroundings. It allows the car to respect road signs, avoid obstacles and locate itself within its environment. The motion sensors, which are integrated in the front and rear bumpers, detect vehicles far in front and behind the car and measure their speed. Depending on the situation, the car accelerates or slows down. They see further and better in rain and fog than the lidar. Another type of sensor acts as an inner ear, giving the car its sense of orientation. The camera, which is located by the interior rear-view mirror, detects and interprets traffic lights, traffic signs and the presence of pedestrians. The lidar, sensors and cameras then transmit the information to the system's brain: a set of different software. After processing the data and evaluating the situation, it makes a decision and controls the actions via servo control on the steering wheel, accelerator and brakes. For a fully autonomous car, all the driver needs to do is give the car its destination via a screen or voice command. For other cars, autonomous mode is deactivated as soon as the steering wheel, pedals or stop button is pressed, depending on the model.

What is the status of autonomous car projects for GAFA (the major players that have opted to partake in this adventure) and car manufacturers? Almost all of them have an autonomous car project, thousands of engineers are working on these projects and billions (of euros and dollars) have been invested, with the objective that a child born today will never need to pass a driving test.

4.3. The medical industry

As the basic level of knowledge required to be a health professional is increasing (it doubles almost every year), a physician is not in an even playing field, with more than 3,000 new articles being indexed every day in the PubMed database (PubMed gathers medical and biological articles). This makes it almost impossible to stay up to date with all the latest medical information. Artificial intelligence is undoubtedly one of the best ways to remedy this problem by analyzing all the available information with the aim of revealing correlations, models, etc., and thus helping doctors to implement the most relevant treatments, protocols, etc. for each type of disease. The advent of connected devices (sensors) and diagnostic aid software are vectors for telemedicine development. Connected devices entirely dedicated to health are now a reality (tensiometer, blood glucose measurement, pill box and so on). For the moment, they are developed independently (proprietary solutions, each device works with its own application) and there is no single (standardized) communication protocol to allow sharing of data in the same format. More generally, the web giants GAFA are investing heavily in predictive medicine (we will see to what end). Current curative medicine (which only treats a disease when it has manifested itself) could be replaced in the medium term by predictive medicine that is based on connected devices (Big Data) and Artificial Intelligence (analysis of Big Data). With the objective of having a more predictive and personalized medicine, it is likely that we will witness a revolution in terms of health in the coming decades. People at risk of disease will be equipped with medical surveillance devices (connected sensors) and connected to the Internet of Things. These connected devices will enable real-time retrieval of medical and health information from patient monitoring, which will be analyzed via Artificial Intelligence platforms. This could give rise to an "interactive" medicine where the patient is constantly connected to a virtual doctor.

Figure 4.4. *Connected medicine*

4.4. "Smart" personal assistant (or agent)

A "smart" personal assistant (or a bot, which is the contraction of robot) is in fact an application that has the function of helping us in our daily tasks. Its main features are as follows:

– a certain degree of autonomy, which remains under the control of the user, who alone decides the level of delegation of the task;

– the ability to act and/or react to one's environment during the execution of an activity where the context might have changed (for example, having to change a password that has expired, informing the user and guiding him through the process);

– the ability to collaborate with other software assistants or humans;

– the capacity to learn, which will constantly improve the performance of a task.

In summary, we could say that an intelligent personal assistant must have knowledge (access to the information necessary for a task) and must act on this knowledge (update it). It must be able to examine its objectives (such as managing a calendar), plan its actions (in relation to its objectives) and possibly act on its plans. In addition, it must be able to interact with other assistants. This linking of smart assistants (whether personal or not – integrated into the web) will be the source of a new evolution in Internet usage. We will enter a new area of the Web, and may even speak of an Intelligent Internet that will be more proactive, with better knowledge (explicit or implicit) of its users.

There are several types of smart assistants (personal and non-personal) that have the ability to:

– communicate with other assistants;

– act within an environment;

– understand the user's environment;

– provide services.

Smart assistants will soon become part of our daily lives. Stakeholders such as the Google Assistant, Apple with Siri, Microsoft with Cortana and many others are developing their own intelligent personal assistants. These assistants have one thing in common: machine learning. From the information that we make available to them and the information they acquire by themselves, these assistants are able to assist us (through recommendations, advice, etc.). They will be increasingly present in our homes (as support for home automation[2]). Voice will be the main method of communication between us and them, allowing them to recognize who is who. All the functions that we currently perform on our smartphones (making appointments, managing your calendar, booking a concert, ordering a meal, etc.) can be done by these assistants, who will become actual

---

2 From Wikipedia: "Home automation or domotics is building automation for a home, called a smart home or smart house. It involves the control and automation of lighting, heating (such as smart thermostats), ventilation, air conditioning (HVAC) and security, as well as home appliances such as washer/dryers, ovens or refrigerators/freezers".

assistants (for the family or individual) with the ability to correlate information that will enable them to anticipate changes and risks related to the task (and therefore the objective to be achieved). For example, for an appointment that requires a journey, the smart assistant will have the ability to analyze the state of traffic in real-time, duration of the trip, possible options, etc. in order to foresee a change in context that could impact the appointment early enough. Recent studies show that a large majority (>90 %) of smartphone users have already used a personal assistant (Siri, Google Now, Ok Google...).

Figure 4.5. *A smart assistant in a smart home*

4.5. Image and sound recognition

Image is revolutionizing communication on the Internet, with several billions of images shared daily on various social networks, which has the effect of making the Internet more and more visual, and by capillarity, changing its uses. Images are replacing words. It is no longer enough for actors on the web (brands...) to analyze "words"; they also need to be able to decipher images. Image recognition applications do not stop at marketing, and they encompass disciplines such as facial recognition, robotics, translation and advertising.

The following steps are (in summary) needed to learn a neural network:

1) gathering the learning data is one of the most structuring and time-consuming steps. It involves collecting all the data that will be needed to create (and validate) the model;

2) modeling will define the characteristics of the target model. It requires extracting the variables that are relevant for the model (feature engineering[3]): geometric shapes, the main colors in an image, etc. This is a crucial step because the quality of these variables will depend on the relevance of the model. This step will also be used to determine the characteristics of the neural network (type and number of layers). This step could be qualified as "technical" in the analytical sense of the word;

3) configuration of the network and its settings (between the learning data and those necessary for validation);

4) the learning phase is the step that aims to feed the model with data (learning and validation), to train it and verify it. Adjustments will be made by comparing the prediction of the model (output) with the expected result;

5) the output (prediction) is the last step, where we consider whether the model is reliable, well trained and therefore operational.

---

3 Features such as shapes, colors, etc.

Neural networks are organized into successive, hierarchical layers, each dedicated to a task, with the principle that the deeper one moves into the network, the more complex the task is to carry out. For image recognition, first we identify pixels, which are used to define colors, contours, then increasingly complex shapes, and finally a face, an object and an animal.

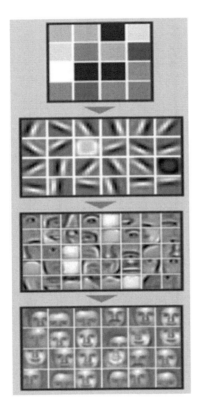

Layer 1: the machine detects the light and dark pixels

Layer 2: the machine learns to identify simple shapes

Layer 3: the machine learns to identify complex shapes

Layer 4: the machine learns to identify which shapes can be used to define a human face

Figure 4.6. *In this example of facial recognition, the layers are hierarchized. They start at the top layer and the tasks get increasingly complex*

Figure 4.7. *The same technique can be used for augmented reality (perception of the environment), placing it on-board a self-driving vehicle to provide information to the automatic control of the vehicle*

4.6. Recommendation tools

The objective of recommendation tools is to increase the commercial efficiency of an e-commerce website by improving the conversion rate (relationship between the number of visitors and the number of buyers), which is one of the key indicators for management to know if the products (goods or services) offered to Internet users correspond to their expectations. Very early on, major players in the online sector used the recommendation principle to suggest products to visitors, products that were in line with their profile and/or the contents already in their shopping basket. One way to improve the conversion rate or increase the average shopping cart is to offer products bought by other users (with a similar profile), articles related to the product being viewed or products recommended by other Internet users. There are innumerable possibilities for suggesting products to a visitor. The implementation of such cross-selling or up-selling strategies is far from simple. Referral algorithms are fed with navigation data, the profile of the user (explicit or implicit) and the company's strategy (what products should be "pushed" in which context, see Figure 4.8).

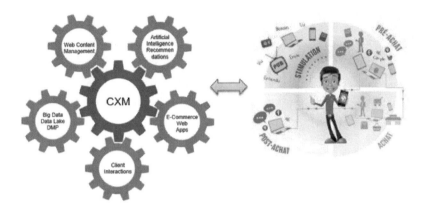

Figure 4.8. *Recommendations are integrated into the customer path through the right channel. Customer contact channels tend to multiply rather than replace each other, forcing companies to adapt their communications to each channel (content format, interaction, language, etc.). The customer wishes to choose their channel and be able to change it depending on the circumstances (time of day, location, subject of interest, expected results, etc.)*

4.6.1. *Collaborative filtering (a "collaborative" recommendation mode)*

Collaborative filtering is the set of methods that builds recommendation systems using the opinions and assessments of a group to help users with their choices. The purpose of collaborative filtering is to offer users products (goods or services) that may be of interest to them. There are several ways to build these recommendations: the simplest way is based on declarative data while the most complex way is based on users' browsing data: pages visited, frequency of visits, basket content (product association...), visit duration and, of course, votes left by users on different products. So once again, data are what makes the difference. Collaborative filtering is based on an exchange system between Internet users; we could speak of a "digital word of mouth" that is made possible because of the Internet and platforms that make rating or commenting systems available. Major online players have largely contributed to the deployment of these techniques, which is very simple for the declarative part: it requires associating the customer with a product and a score (or a like). The aim is therefore to predict a customer's desire for a product that he has not yet purchased in order to suggest one that is most likely to meet his expectations. Collaborative filtering is based on customer interactions produced in several ways:

– *Declarative*, with or without presence of purchase, is a so-called neighborhood method based on indices of similarity (correlation) between customers and the products they like or buy. The principle is based on the assumption that customers with similar preferences will appreciate products in a similar way.

- Advantages: a large amount of data is available (even all the navigation data of clients, as well as their "recommendations", likes, etc.);

- Disadvantages: this is only declarative and has not necessarily been verified by a purchase.

– *Modeled* has the same principle as for the declarative form, but solely based on purchasing acts.

- Advantages: correlations are based on facts (purchasing actions) and not just a declared preference;

- Disadvantages: the volume of available data (a few %) is rather low (in light of the number of visits to the e-commerce website).

– *Hybrid*, whereby the two previous methods (declarative and modeled) are joined, makes it possible to link the advantages of each method while limiting the disadvantages.

One of the assumptions made when implementing collaborative filtering is that the Internet user needs to be recognized either formally (via accesses on the e-commerce website) or informally (via open data: IP address, device ID (identification number of the device), cookies, etc.) in order to be able to build the customer profile and propose products that would suit the customer best.

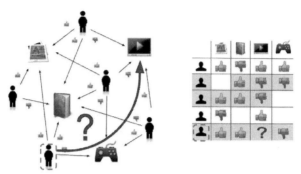

We seek to know if this Internet user would be interested in movies, by comparing him to people who "look like him".

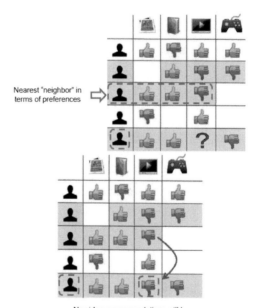

Nearest "neighbor" in terms of preferences

No video recommendations will be suggested to this user

Figure 4.9. *Collaborative filtering, step by step. In this example, we can see that the closest "neighbor" in terms of preferences is not interested in videos, which will inform the recommendation engine about the (possible) preferences of the Internet user (in this case, do not recommend videos). If the user is interested in video products, models (based on self-learning) will take this into account when browsing, and their profile will be "boosted" by this information*

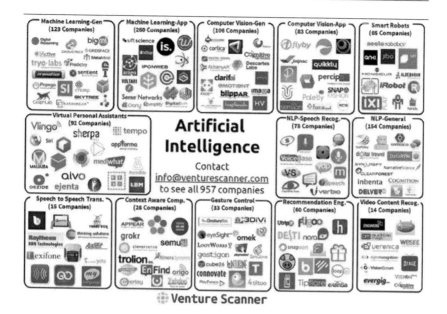

Figure 4.10. *Mapping of start-ups in the world of Artificial Intelligence*

Conclusion

Can one really conclude a story that has only just begun?

Digital trends have allowed us to quite confidently predict that no sector will be left untouched by Artificial Intelligence. The big advantage of these self-learning algorithms is that they can learn from all types of data, making their scope unlimited. Their main strengths are their ability to learn, whereas a computer program is programmed to accomplish a task. Automatic learning algorithms alleviate this problem, in that they are able to learn how to perform tasks based on the data available to them using pattern recognition[1]. The more data these algorithms have, the more they can correlate and automatically build a program that is applicable to new data. These algorithms have been used for years already to search for information on the Internet, automatically categorize e-mails (spam), or recommend products or people likely to be of interest to the user.

Strong Artificial Intelligence remains heavily debated: imagine a machine that could be self-conscious, could analyze its own reasoning, has emotions. Some believe that a sufficiently well-programmed and powerful machine could

---

1 This could be translated as shape or signal recognition.

not only simulate intelligent behavior (carrying out any "intelligent" task that can be done by a human), but could also experience a real awareness of itself, "real feelings" and understand its own reasoning. Today, consciousness has a material medium that is biological (neurons). The question would be: from the moment we can reproduce the functioning of neurons, is it possible to consider a material support that would not be biological (like computers)? Nothing is stopping us from thinking about it, all that remains is to invent a computer that has an architecture organized around artificial neurons (or another support) that would interconnect 100 billion neurons. The first step in this process will undoubtedly be the development of increasingly more powerful companion robots (some are already available), filled with sensors (cameras, microphones, electrostatic, infrared, pressure, acceleration, vibration and temperature sensors, etc.), that will enable them to understand their environment. Algorithms will make it possible to recognize faces (knowing who is who), languages (what is being said – voice command will undoubtedly be a key communication vector between the robot and a human), devices (what the surroundings are) and adapt their behavior to meet the expectations of each person, to react to situations (such as fire, noise and intrusion) and/or to carry out tasks that will be allocated to it.

A crucial point for Artificial Intelligence, which is its core foundation, is self-learning, and its ability to learn from its experiences but also to remember its past actions.

Artificial Intelligence remains a wild discipline in need of taming. The field has not yet existed for long enough to allow us to assert that algorithms (based on neural networks) that are associated with Big Data, which are already available (through the Internet) or will become available via the IoT, telemedicine, home automation, etc., are or will not be "harmful", or at the very least trap us in a system where all our behaviors, preferences, choices, etc., are turned into equations. This would mean that our lives would be under the control of algorithms (nowadays, neural networks are true black boxes). Another approach would be to say that Artificial Intelligence can be put at the service of the human being; within the framework of medicine, it will allow us to improve prevention, diagnosis and even adapt treatment to the patient. It will have an impact on the way we work, communicate, organize our lives. It will free us from tasks where a machine is more efficient than human, which will allow us to concentrate on our cognitive capacities such as creativity, innovation and so on, with the bet that the machine is and will remain at the service of humanity and not the other way around.

Within companies, (weak) Artificial Intelligence is probably the only way to efficiently exploit Big Data, as existing Business Intelligence (BI) solutions are overwhelmed by the non-stop flow of data (not to mention their different formats). Data Management teams[2] can no longer cope, and analytical profiles are increasingly difficult to recruit. Meanwhile, the temporality of a decision and action is now just milliseconds (with no or little room for long analysis processes).

The question this book is asking is whether algorithms can take over. It is clear that in the next decade, we are going to experience a "diffuse" deployment of Artificial Intelligence (we could speak of pervasive Artificial Intelligence) in our daily lives (professional and private). We will unknowingly use more and more algorithms in our various devices, and our data will be analyzed by more and more machines and we will communicate with them (and they will communicate with each other) without us really realizing that it is not a human being at the other end.

2 Human and material means to collect, store, use and secure a company's data.

Transport, home automation, robotics, medicine, security and many other fields will rely on Artificial intelligence. This "new world" will have good and less good aspects but we will have to coexist with this new form of intelligence. Some will trust it, others will be wary of it, but there is a good chance that it will be part of a form of collective intelligence arising from the digital world.

APPENDICES

Appendix 1

Big Data

As you will probably have realized by now, these are data from our digital world (the Internet), which are continuously produced (the Internet never sleeps) at ever-growing speeds, volumes and formats. The Internet of Things (IoT) will only accentuate this trend. This quantitative explosion of digital data has forced major online players (Yahoo, Google, Amazon, Facebook, etc.), for which data are their "raw material", to imagine new ways of processing and analyzing these massive data (using the computer industry), with the buzz word: time (the power to carry out analyses in near real time). Thus, the concept of Big Data was born.

Ultimately, Big Data is a very large data set that conventional tools (relational or analytical data management engines) or data processing tools (data extraction and transformation) cannot handle in increasingly shorter time frames (almost at the real-time pace of transactional processes).

The volume of available data is growing, and doing so in different formats. However, the cost of storage is decreasing, which makes it very easy to store large volumes of data. However, the problem of processing these data (both in terms of volume and format) is still ongoing; Big Data (through its technical approach) is interested in this last part, whereas Smart Data is more concerned with the analytical dimension, the value and integration of Big Data in the company's decision-making processes. Big Data should be seen as a new data source that the company must integrate and correlate with its existing data, and not as a concept (and associated solutions) that could replace existing Business Intelligence. Big Data adds itself to the range of solutions that companies have put in place for processing, exploiting and disseminating data in order to help them make informed decisions, whether for strategic or operational purposes.

Technological developments have opened up new horizons for data storage and management. This has made it possible to store anything and everything at unbeatable costs (because of the large volumes and little structuring of the data). One difficulty in terms of deriving value is the "noise" generated by data that have not been processed upstream of the storage process (too much data, ultimately "killing" the data), which is a negative aspect. On the positive side though, the storage of "raw" data opens up (or at least does not close) the possibility of making new discoveries from "source" data, which would not have been possible if the data had been processed/filtered before storage. It will therefore be necessary to mediate between these two axes, depending on the objectives that have been set.

A1.1. The four Vs

Big Data is "data" that are mainly characterized by the four Vs: Volume, Variety, Velocity, Veracity followed by a fifth "V" for Value (associated with Smart Data)

– V for "Volume"

In 2014, there were about 3 billion Internet users connected through over 6 billion devices (mainly servers, PCs, tablets, smartphones) using an IP address (Internet Protocol, a "unique" identifier that allows a connected device to be uniquely identified and thus allow communication with its peers) that was mainly for smartphones, tablets and computers. This generated about 8 exabytes of data (10 to the power of 18 = one billion billion bytes) in 2014 alone. A byte is an 8-bit sequence (the bit being the basic unit of computing, represented by a zero or one), which allows the digitization of information. In the very near future, with the advent of connected devices (objects in our daily lives, such as televisions, household appliances, surveillance cameras, etc., which will be connected to the Internet), we will have several tens of billions of such objects (about 50 billion), which could generate more than forty thousand exabytes of data per year (40,000 billion bytes)! Obviously, the Internet is very verbose, with billions of events happening every minute. Some may be of value to a company, some may be relevant, others less so. But to be able to decide this, it is necessary to be able to read them, sort through them... in a single word, to "reduce" these data, going through storage, filtering, organizing and analyzing them.

– V for "Variety"

For a long time, we only had to process highly structured data, often from transactional systems, which once they were extracted and transformed, were loaded into so-called decision-making databases. These databases differ in their data model (or how the data are stored, and the relationships between them).

Transactional data model: in this model (data storage and manipulation structure), the emphasis is on the execution speed of reading, writing and modifying data to minimize the duration of a transaction and maximize the number of actions that can be carried out in parallel (for example an e-commerce website must be able to support thousands of online users that are simultaneously accessing their catalog of available products and prices through selective criteria, with little or no need for access to historical data). This is called a "standardized" data model, which translates into data structures being organized into types/entities (for example customer data are stored in a different structure from product data, or invoices, etc.). This induces little or no redundancy in the data; however, we have to manage the numerous and often complex relationships/links between these entities (which implies very good knowledge of the data model; these actions are delegated to the solutions/applications and are very rarely executed by a business analyst as they are much too complex). In summary, the standardized model allows very high efficiency of transactional activities, but makes it difficult, if not impossible, to implement Business Intelligence solutions (from this data model), other than operational reporting (no or little room for analytics).

Decision data model: in this model, the emphasis is on the analysis and modeling, which requires a great deal of historical information – we are talking about years' worth, with access to a much wider scope of data (for example all products for all seasons, etc.). These constraints have made it difficult, if not impossible, to use relational data models (the links and relationships between entities, associated with volume, have had a huge impact on the execution time of requests). The solution to this problem is to implement destandardized data models. These are models with a much simpler structure (known as "stars" or "snowflakes", which correspond to a set of stars linked by their dimensions) where the data (source) are stored in a single structure that contains all the entities. For example, the customer, the product, the price and the invoice will be stored in the same table (known as the facts table), and are accessible via analysis, wherefrom the set gets its star shape (hence the name). This data model facilitates access (no or few links, apart from those needed for dimension tables), and this access will be much more sequential (although it is indexed). On the other hand, there will be a redundancy of data, due to the way information is stored in the "facts table" (a larger volume to process). Companies have to deal with much less structured (or even unstructured) data, such as messages, blogs, social networks, website logs, movies, photos, etc. These new types of data require special processing (classification, reduction (selecting what is relevant)) in order to be integrated into the company's decision-making solutions.

– V for "velocity"

The Internet and its billions of users generate an uninterrupted stream of activity (the Internet never sleeps) and all these activities (whether commercial, social, cultural, etc.) are managed by software agents such as e-commerce websites, blogs, social networks..., which in turn produce continuous data flows. Companies must be able to process these data in "real-time" (the term "real-time" is always difficult to define but in the context of the Internet, we could say that this time must be aligned with the temporality of the user's session). Companies must be able to act and react (proposing content, products, prices, etc., to meet the expectations of their customers, whatever the time, day or night) in the very competitive context of the Internet. A customer does not (or no longer) belong(s) to a company or brand, the notion of loyalty is becoming less and less clear. Ultimately, the company or the brand only possesses the time that the customer is willing to grant it and in these conditions, it is necessary to always be able to satisfy the customer's expectations.

– V for "value" (associated with Smart Data)

What value can be derived from Big Data?

This is the crux of the matter: what applies to Big Data is true for all data. We could say that data without value (that is not be exploited) is reduced to data that has a cost (its processing, storage, etc.). The value of the data therefore lies in its use. Companies are well aware that they are far from exploiting all the data available to them (they are mainly focused on highly structured data from transactional systems). Globalization, combined with the (inflationary) digitalization of our world, has accentuated this awareness, competition has become tougher, opportunities are greater and the ability to "know" before acting is a real advantage. Big Data follows the same rule, it must be seen as an additional source of information (structured and unstructured) that will enrich a company's decision-making processes (technical and human): this is the "crucible" where Big Data begins its transformation into Smart Data.

Appendix 2

Smart Data

Smart Data represents the way in which different data sources (including Big Data) are reconciled, correlated, analyzed, etc., in order to feed into the decision-making and action-taking processes. A lot of data are "Big" (in terms of volume, velocity), but how many are "Smart" (valuable for the company)?

Smart Data must be thought of as a set of technologies, processes and the associated organization (Business Intelligence Competence Centers) that enable us to extract value from data. It is based on Business Intelligence. Smart Data is one of the fundamental cores of Business Intelligence (whether analytical or operational) and has developed, driven by Business Intelligence "2.0" toward a number of new features such as more formal integration into business processes (within business processes) where the necessary information is disseminated at all levels of a company and the decision must made be as closely as possible to its implementation (action). Business management and optimization indicators are aligned with operational decision-making and action-taking processes. Operational departments quickly appropriated this new generation of tools, taking their operational rather than analytical approaches into account. This has allowed a simpler alignment of company management through common and measurable indicators and objectives (Key Performance Indicators). The organization around Business Intelligence has aligned itself with this approach, with a much more transversal role, thus Business Intelligence Competency Centers (BICCs) saw the light of day. Globalization has led to the decentralization of decision-making poles and the rampant digitization of our environment and therefore requires decision-making and action-taking processes to be carried out without delay. Coupling is stronger with transactional solutions. The Internet has changed the landscape in terms of decision-making and action-taking cycles, and the digitization of transactional processes (e-commerce websites, etc.) has facilitated the integration and flow between these two worlds: the transactional world (operational activities) and the decision-making world (analytical activities). This coupling required drastically reducing the duration of the "decision-making" cycle, which consists of data capturing and transformation, storage and analysis, and publication (to feed the cycle of decisions and actions).

Here are a few examples to support this.

Recommendation engines appear on e-commerce websites. These software agents interact in real time (within the context and session of a user), based on statistical analyses enriched by the transactional context, in order to make recommendations (different products, prices, etc. can be proposed within the transactional process itself, depending on the user's navigation path or the knowledge we have of the user's preferences). For the implementation of its rules, the recommendation engine will use:

– analytical data on segmentations, scores, appetences;

– transactional context data, navigation path;

– event alerts: it is very easy to be notified if an event takes place (such as follow-up on a delivery, step by step...), or even to automate a certain number of actions related to an event.

In terms of payment security, a real-time credit card purchase can be validated or not thanks to (self-learning) risk algorithms for fraud detection, which limit the risk of non-payment for companies. All these examples were made possible by linking reconciled transactional events to decision data, which are all orchestrated by rules/recommendation engines. The mobility and temporality of information from new devices, such as tablets or smartphones, combined with increasingly efficient networks (Wi-Fi, 4G) have become the key vectors of this new "informational space-time" through a near-permanent connection to the Internet (or to internal networks within companies) linked to wireless communication modes. The link between information and those who consume it (strategic, operational decision makers, or simply Internet users) is never broken, which makes it possible to make a good decision with the right information at the right time and in the right context. The information has had to adapt to these new formats (advent of responsive/adaptive design, or the capacity for informational content to adapt to the technical presentation constraints of various devices). The temporality of data processing (capture, analysis, restitution) has been aligned with that of the business processes for which the information is intended (this is crucial as it implies good knowledge of business processes). This new mode of operation has required changes to the Information System (IS) through its urbanization (managing communication between IS components) to allow "real-time" processing of information. This IS urbanization model is known as event-oriented architecture, which aims to "urbanize" the data, moving toward systems that consume it in real time.

With the automation of analyses, the Internet never really sleeps (online activity is permanent, it is always daytime somewhere in the world). Tools and analysis cycles have had to adapt to this new time frame (in the past, companies used the period of "non-activity", usually night time, for data processing and updating decision support systems but with the Internet of today, this mode of operation is less and less effective, if even at all). The processes of analyzing, modeling, segmenting data, etc. have been automated: they have become self-learning (able to integrate new information they receive along the way) and are then used by transactional applications (via rules/recommendation engines). This has divided the analytical processes into the following:

– Operational analysis (to support transactional solutions) features automated "operational" analytical processing. Human intervention remains limited to: controlling and monitoring the correct application of rules and/or the consistency of models through tools integrated into the analytical platform. Over time, transactional information (such as web page visits, product/price queries, purchases, etc.) enriches the databases, models, etc. used by rule/recommendation engines.

– Exploratory analysis (location of construction, research, etc.): this is a more traditional analytical mode, where analysts/statisticians analyze data to draw new conclusions that will enrich the operational analysis. These two modes are complementary. Exploratory analysis (analytical) focuses on the discovery and construction of models (for example purchasing behavior, customer segmentation, palatability scores, etc.), which will then be used (in real time) and are enriched during the operational analysis.

– The organizational dimension: in order to implement and exploit Big and Smart Data, companies should have an adequate BI structure. It will be responsible for implementing and supporting the company's Business

Intelligence strategy. The BICC is an organizational support. The aim of BICC is to be a transversal organizational structure (across the whole company, to break away from the "silos" approach of needs and Business Intelligence solutions) that encompasses three profiles:

- technical profiles, which ensure the technological dimensions (tools, database, etc.) in terms of implementation and support, quality of data processing management, etc.;

- analytical profiles, which ensure analysis and transcription of business needs, data analysis, business data analysis training;

- business profiles, which ensure there is a link with the company's strategy and related business needs.

– Alignment (of processes and organization) between indicators and business processes, and change in management (related to new tools, processes, etc.): ensuring the implementation and monitoring of a BI master plan for the company, implementing a multiyear roadmap that is in line with the operational and strategic needs of a company, anticipating developments around BI (tools, new trends, etc.) and setting up a monitoring unit.

– Optimization investments around decision-making projects.

– Ensuring coherence of BI projects and pooling resources (technical and human): Ensuring the implementation and monitoring of a data governance program: defining BI standards and norms for the company and ensuring user training, whether in terms of tools or data.

Big Data strives to produce a large volume of transactional data (purchasing activity, browsing a website, etc.) at a very high velocity (almost in real time). In order not to alter this velocity, data processing must be limited. In barely a few seconds, it is not possible to capture, process and model navigation data from an e-commerce website that may have thousands of connected users, and then interact with them in real time (in the context of the user's session) to make a recommendation... On the other hand, extracting necessary data from this navigation (transaction by transaction) to contextualize in real time (for example country of origin, page/products already consulted, number of visits, etc. via cookies and/or a tag placed on the page) will allow the process of recommendations, management of rules, etc. to retrieve the right information from Smart Data (behavioral/purchase models, customer segment, etc.) in order to optimize the action taken (for example recommendation of an alternative product, etc.).

Appendix 3

Data Lakes

A data lake is a new way of organizing and storing data, which is linked to the current architecture around Big Data. The idea is to be able to store any format and granularity of data ("raw" or transformed data). The aim of a data lake is not to limit data analysis to a predefined format or scheme (which is more or less the case for existing analytical databases), but to allow analysts and systems that consume the data (automated analytical processes) to have access to the source data without any "filter" (thus determining its use). The goal is to increase the flexibility and speed of implementation of various data projects or initiatives.

How are data lakes different from existing analytical solutions (such as data marts and data warehouses[1]?

One of the fundamental differences is in the database structure:

– Data marts or data warehouses have predefined data models (enforced storage scheme) and these data models aim to store the transformed data in a predefined format (indicators, dimensions, etc.) and shape (physical format)

---

1 A data warehouse is a warehouse that stores all of a company's data (for analysis). A data mart is a subject-oriented data warehouse (for example a client data mart), which is often seen as a subset of the data warehouse.

during the modeling of the database. The tools for this transformation are called Extract Transform Loads[2]. Therefore, in this case, *the data are structured at the moment of its "writing"* in the target database (data mart or data warehouse), and any source data that have not been integrated into the target database will not be accessible to users (analysts or systems that consume these data). Of course, the limitations of this type of data architecture and all new requirements will have to be analyzed by technical teams (feasibility, planning, costs, etc.) for an implementation that could prove to be onerous. This is especially the case for historical data (sources) that need to be recovered according to the new target data model. For each new change, this process has to be iterated. Users are effectively "tied by their hands and feet" to IT departments (or analytical solution providers). This is a real hindrance to exploration, innovation, agility... It is mainly these limitations that have forced architects to rethink data storage.

– The data lake has opened up new horizons for data analysis. Adapting to a digital environment that is perpetually in motion in an ever-tighter temporality is the key. We must be able to interact in real time. This goes beyond the Business Intelligence aspect of existing analytical solutions, since value creation is no longer limited to just using data for reporting purposes, but also and above all using it for much more operational purposes such as interaction with transactional processes (artificial intelligence solutions

---

2 From Wikipedia: "In computing, extract, transform, load (ETL) refers to a process in database usage and especially in data warehousing. [...] Data extraction is where data are extracted from homogeneous or heterogeneous data sources; data transformation where the data are transformed for storing in the proper format or structure for the purposes of querying and analysis; data loading where the data are loaded into the final target database, more specifically, an operational data store, data mart or data warehouse".

are a good example). One of the main advantages of a data lake is that it does not impose any scheme on the data during storage, resulting in a situation where one may have to manage unstructured data, which could potentially have an impact on quality (complexity in setting up data qualification processes due to their lack of structure). The exploitation of data in a data lake differs from data marts or data warehouses in that the *structuring of the data takes place at the time of reading*, so the analyst or system that consumes the data must know what it is looking for when reading the data. We could take this data lake metaphor a step further by saying that the net size and mesh size will determine what kind of fish we want to catch. This approach of structuring during reading is only applied to the data when it is used, thus allowing the source data to be preserved in its original state and preserving the analysis potential. The downside of this approach is the need to develop considerably more skills in terms of tools and understanding than before (tools are distinctly more technical, knowledge and understanding of source data needs to be "sharper"). The richness of integrated data lake management platforms allows data scientists to take advantage of the data and quickly build analytical scenarios. Machine learning processes are also very often associated with it, as they aim to exploit all the available data to constitute interworking and self-learning analytical solutions.

In the vast majority of cases, the implementation of a data lake occurs at a time when a company begins to ask itself questions about its existing analytical infrastructure. Business units need to improve the way they use their data by simplifying its availability (through centralization of sources) and accelerating innovation cycles. The media and marketing industry has pioneered the implementation of data lakes (for customer interaction analysis purposes). This has resulted in the implementation of a Data Management

Platform[3] (DMP) that integrates a data lake. These data are then fed into analytical solutions (machine learning or standard analytical processes) that will allow us to act or react during the contact cycle or purchase cycle. It is a field of application that is opening up a little more every day (IoT, traceability, security). The massive collection capacity and volumes of information produced by the rampant digitization of our world proposes new fields of application for these technologies, allowing us to apprehend huge masses of data and automate their use (artificial intelligence will undoubtedly play a significant role here).

3 It involves retrieving, centralizing, managing and using data relative to prospective and customer interactions. The first DMPs focused on Internet browsing data and were used for behavioral advertizing. Now, the most advanced DMPs integrate various points of contact for data collection and targeted marketing.

Appendix 4

Some Vocabulary Relevant to Artificial Intelligence[1]

Agent: an autonomous unit (or entity) that is capable of representation, action and communication. In the field of artificial intelligence, the agent is a robot or computer program that has the ability to perceive its environment, generally via sensors, and to act according to this perception and its rules. There are several types of agents that work in defined environments. A conversational agent is based on algorithms for processing language: this is its domain. Multiagent systems consist of several agents acting together in a given domain (see Distributed Artificial Intelligence).

Adaptive algorithm: an algorithm that is capable of modifying responses or processed data according to how its environment changes. In contrast to a deterministic algorithm, an adaptive algorithm is called non-deterministic or probabilistic. Two executions of the same adaptive algorithm can give different choices.

Artificial Intelligence: several definitions may apply to AI. It is defined by one of its creators, Marvin Lee Minsky, as "the construction of computer programs that engage in tasks that are, for now, more satisfactorily accomplished by

---

1 Source: journaldunet.com (JDN).

humans because they require high-level mental processes such as perceptual learning, the organization of memory and critical thinking". By extension, AI is a scientific discipline that encompasses manufacturing methods and engineering of so-called intelligent machines and programs. The aim of AI is to produce autonomous machines that are capable of performing complex tasks using reflective processes similar to those of humans.

Automatic learning (or machine learning): branch of artificial intelligence that is focused on learning processes that allow a machine to evolve without its algorithms being modified. There are several types of learning machine: statistical, supervised (where learning rules are defined from a base of examples) or unsupervised.

Bayesian: this is a probability calculation based on the theorem of the British mathematician Thomas Bayes. In artificial intelligence, Bayesian inference is a reasoning that allows us to deduce the probability of whether an event will occur or not.

Bayesian networks: a probabilistic graph representation, or language, that expresses the certainty or uncertainty of an inference. Bayesian networks are based on the British mathematician Thomas Bayes' formula linking probabilities via nodes. Nodes contain the name of a variable and a table of probabilities or propositions associated with this variable according to parent values.

Cognitive science: it deals with the multidisciplinary field of research on the mechanisms and functioning of mental processes. Cognitive science seeks to describe the mechanisms of human thought, consciousness and intelligence, with a view to reproducing them in computer systems. This science brings together several disciplines such as psychology, linguistics, neuroscience and computer science.

Conversational agent or chatbot: human-machine interface that manages the interaction between humans and an agent via a dialog. Chatbots are based on exchanges in natural language. The system interprets the user's expressions and provides answers that are also in natural language. Conversational agent technology is based on the language processing industry.

Decision tree: graphical representation (in the shape of a tree) of the rules used in the decision-making process. The decision tree consists of decision nodes and branches. It is used in machine learning and allows different results to be calculated depending on the decision taken. It also makes predictions based on probabilities.

Deep learning: a machine learning method that is part of the "automatic learning" field of artificial intelligence. Deep learning allows unsupervised learning. It is based on the analysis of a data model. It is particularly suitable for image recognition or natural language processing.

Distributed Artificial Intelligence (DAI): a branch of artificial intelligence that aims to create decentralized systems, usually multiagents, that are capable of cooperating and coordinating. Distributed artificial intelligence studies techniques that allow autonomous agents to interact with each other, and the means of distributing a problem among them. These techniques are inspired by the complex structures of certain insect societies such as ants. One of the areas of application of DAI is the coordination of autonomous mobile agents (such as airplanes or cars), which must learn to avoid each other while experiencing travel and being under time constraints.

Expert system: a system for solving problems based on a set of rules that have been recorded previously in a knowledge base and relate to a restricted area. It is relevant in weak Artificial Intelligence. Like an expert in the field, the system applies rules and is said to be deterministic. If a system does not have rules to process a specific case, it is inoperative. Expert systems have proven their worth in highly-targeted areas where the knowledge base is sufficient to handle all possible cases. An expert system generally consists of a knowledge base, an inference engine and a rule base.

Fuzzy logic: reasoning that includes all the intermediate possibilities between true or false values. Conventional logic of deterministic computer systems, i.e. those outside the domain of AI, is based on true or false values, which are equivalent to yes or no for humans. Humans and AI are capable of handling fuzzy logic and also integrating a number of nuances between these values, such as values that are often or rarely interspersed between the values always and never.

Heuristics: it refers to problem-solving methods that are based on past results. Heuristics does not rely on formal modeling and does not necessarily guarantee effective responses. According to computer scientists Newell, Shaw and Simon, heuristics are processes "that may solve a given problem, but offer no guarantee of doing so". In short, the system has to choose between several possibilities without any certainty that its choice is the right one.

Inference or reasoning: this is a deduction operation from implicit information. Like logic, it is the basis of all reasoning. Inference is used to create links between information in order to derive an assertion, conclusion or hypothesis. It uses a set of rules based on a reference system.

Knowledge base: a collection of information relating to a given topic. A knowledge base includes all the knowledge that an expert in the field must master in order to be able to exercise his or her expertise. This is particularly used in expert systems.

Logic: this is the science of reasoning and the application or expression of reasoning. Along with representation and reasoning, or inference, logic is the third factor in the triptych of a system's ability to deduce. There are several types of logic: propositional logic, first order logic, etc.

Modeling: consists of developing models from information to simulate complex systems. These can refer to situations or objects. The purpose of AI modeling is to inform the system that uses it about the situation and functioning of the modeled object.

Natural language: language used by humans as opposed to formal or machine language. Natural language is the medium of oral and written communication in humans.

Neural networks: a program made up of algorithms related to the way the human brain works. Neural networks thus mimic the functioning of the human brain: each function of the program is linked to the others, and information is distributed throughout the network.

Perception: the ability of a system to receive stimuli related to an object or event within its environment. These stimuli, or information, are perceived through a sensor device. Analysis of the data from these stimuli allows the system to characterize the object or environment. This is used in facial recognition, for example.

Predictive analysis: a set of data and statistical analysis technologies that are designed to give predictions, or predictive assumptions, and/or statistical models of events that are likely to occur. Predictive analysis is increasingly used within companies, for example in marketing, to predict consumer behavior.

Probabilities: a branch of mathematics that studies phenomena subjected to chance and uncertainty. In the field of Artificial Intelligence, its aim is to create probabilistic reasoning systems, as opposed to deterministic systems.

Representation of knowledge: a branch of artificial intelligence that deals with information representation models, or knowledge models, to form hypotheses and generate inferences. The knowledge is classified by typology: always true (a square is a polygon with four sides), uncertain/certain, changing...

Robotics: the branch of AI that deals with the design and manufacturing of robots. These machines can be humanoid or automatons as in industry, for example. Robotics relies on other AI disciplines and on mechanical, electrical, hydraulic and other forms of engineering to build robots.

Rules: a knowledge representation format that is computer-operable in a knowledge base. It is used in expert systems and the rules are represented in the form of if (premise) and then (conclusion).

Scheduling and planning: the ability of a system to control another system and react in real time. Scheduling and planning is based on the control system's ability to evaluate a situation or event, make decisions and plan tasks. For example, a scheduling and planning system was able to control a 24-h space shuttle without human intervention.

Strong artificial intelligence: this is the ability of a machine to not only reproduce intelligent thinking and interaction skills (analysis, reasoning, rational action), but also of having a "consciousness", "feelings" and understanding one's own reasoning. Strong AI is a controversial subject, and according to critics, strong AI assumes that the machine "thinks" it knows what it "feels" and knows what it feels. In short, it is gifted with consciousness, which is said to be inaccessible to a system, no matter how complex it may be. Some define strong AI by its ability to solve complex problems in any environment at a level equal to or greater than human intelligence.

Turing test: invented by the British mathematician Alan Turing in 1950, it is intended to evaluate the intelligence of a machine or system. In concrete terms, Turing sought to test the ability of a system to pretend to be a human through a conversation in natural language. The test is carried out anonymously between a human operator, another human and a machine using terminals. Through textual exchanges, the operator must guess which of the interlocutors is a machine.

Weak artificial intelligence: refers to the operation of a system that simulates intelligent behavior in a restricted area.

Appendix 5

Comparison Between Machine Learning and Traditional Business Intelligence

Below is a comparative table between traditional Business Intelligence, where analytical models are built from historical data (historical regression model), and Machine Learning, supervised or not, with a self-learning principle.

	Traditional BI (static approach, not/not well connected to transactional systems)	Machine Learning (dynamic approach, interconnected with transactional systems)
Prerequisites	A sample of the data that is representative of what we are trying to predict.	The system must be connected to its environment (to interact with it).
Model: Objectives	Statisticians know what they are looking for in the data.	Objectives are determined (for example a purchase, an amount, clicks...).
Model: Training	The model is initialized from past data.	Depending on the mode. Supervised: the system is trained with a large volume of data.

		Unsupervised: the system discovers by itself and adjusts its decisions as it learns.
Model: Updating	Statisticians must reset the models with new data (and/or "explanatory" variables) to update the models.	The system is self-learning, it will adapt between action and reaction in a closed loop principle.

Appendix 6

Conceptual Outline of the Steps Required to Implement a Customization Solution based on Machine Learning

1) The first step is to identify a customer through the different contact channels (e-commerce website, mobile application, call center, etc.) and any formal interaction (through formal authentication/identification) or anonymous interaction (no authentication/identification).

2) This step involves identifying which point in the customer buying cycle the user is at: (i) prospective customer who has an interest, (ii) helping them to find the information they need, (iii) initiating a commitment phase (such as registering for a newsletter), (iv) recognizing expectations and preferences, (v) individualizing the relationship, (vi) facilitating access to services (mobile application, dematerialization, etc.) and (vii) allowing the user to share his or her experience.

3) Personalize messages, contents, products, etc. in line with the profile and the customer's expectations through all channels of contact. This phase is crucial as it is the keystone of the personalization strategy.

4) All contact channels need to be integrated both technically and in terms of a proposal (consistency of services across the board). This will ensure the integrity of messages and content throughout the customer journey.

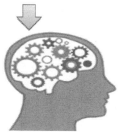

5) A customization solution must be implemented, based on a self-learning system (Machine Learning), which will be the analytical building block of the process.

6) Interactions with customers, regardless of the contact channel, have to be made available in real time for the analytical solution (via a data lake). This will allow for self-learning.

Bibliography

References cited in the text

[BAU 88] BAUM E.B., WILCZEK F., "Supervised learning of probability distributions by neural networks", *Neural Information Processing Systems*, vol. 12, pp. 52–61, 1988.

[BIS 06] BISHOP C.M., *Pattern Recognition and Machine-Learning*, Springer, Berlin, 2006.

[COR 02] CORNUÉJOLS A., MICLET L., KODRATOFF Y., *Apprentissage Artificiel: Concepts et Algorithmes*, Eyrolles, Paris, 2002.

[IAF 15] IAFRATE F., *From Big Data to Smart Data*, ISTE Ltd, London and John Wiley & Sons, New York, 2015.

[KNE 91] KNERR S., Une méthode nouvelle de création automatique de réseaux de neurones pour la classification de données : application à la reconnaissance de chiffres manuscrits, PhD thesis, Pierre and Marie Curie University, Paris, 1991.

[KNE 92] KNERR S., PERSONNAZ L., DREYFUS G., "Handwritten digit recognition by neural networks with Single-layer Training", *IEEE Transactions on Neural Networks*, vol. 3, pp. 962–968, 1992.

[LEW 14] LEWIS M., *Flash Boys*, W.W. Norton, London, 2014.

[MIT 97] MITCHELL T., *Machine Learning*, McGraw-Hill, New York, 1997.

[MON 99] MONARI G., Sélection de modèles non linéaires par leave-one-out; étude théorique et application des réseaux de neurones au procédé de soudage par points, PhD thesis, Pierre and Marie Curie University, Paris, 1999. Available online: http://www.neurones.espci.fr.

[OUS 98] OUSSAR Y., Réseaux d'ondelettes et réseaux de neurones pour la modélisation statique et dynamique de processus, PhD thesis, Pierre and Marie Curie University, Paris, 1998. Available online: http://www.neurones.espci.fr.

[ROU 01] ROUSSEL P., MONCET F., BARRIEU B., VIOLA A., "Modélisation d'un processus dynamique à l'aide de réseaux de neurones bouclés: Application à la modélisation de la relation pluie-hauteur d'eau dans un réseau d'assainissement et à la détection de défaillances de capteurs", *4th International Conference on Innovative technologies in urban drainage*, vol. 1, pp. 919–926, 2001.

[TAN 06] TAN P.N., STEINBACH M., KUMAR V., *Introduction to Data Mining*, Addison Weasley, Boston, 2006.

[VAP 95] VAPNIK V., *The Nature of Statistical Learning Theory*, Springer, Berlin, 1995.

[WOL 00] WOLINSKI F., VICHOT F., STRICKER M., "Using learning-based filters to detect rule-based filtering obsolescence", OAIR 2000, Paris, 2000.

[ZIP 49] ZIPF G.K., *Human Behavior and the Principle of Least Effort*, Addison-Wesley, Boston, 1949.

General bibliography

Technical aspects

TURING A., GIRARD J.-Y., *La machine de Turing, Les Ordinateurs et l'Intelligence*, pp. 133–174, Le Seuil, Paris, 1995.

REMY C., *L'Intelligence artificielle*, Dunod, Paris, 1994.

ALLIOT J.-M., SCHIEX T., *Intelligence artificielle et informatique théorique*, Cepadues, Toulouse, 2002.

GENESERETH M.R., NILSSON N.J., *Logical Foundations of Artificial Intelligence*, Morgan Kaufman, Burlington, 1987.

RUSSELL S.J., NORVIG P., *Intelligence Artificielle*, Pearson Education, New York, 2006.

LAURIERE J.-L., *Intelligence Artificielle*, Eyrolles, Paris, 1986.

DELAHAYE J.-P., *Outils logiques pour l'intelligence artificielle*, Eyrolles, Paris, 1987.

HATON J.-P., HATON M.-C., *L'Intelligence Artificielle*, Presses Universitaires de France, Paris, 1990.

Philosophical aspects

BOSS G., *Les machines à penser - L'homme et l'ordinateur*, Éditions du Grand Midi, Quebec, 1987.

BOLO J., *Philosophie contre intelligence artificielle*, Lingua Franca, Giyan, 1996.

ANDERSON A.R., *Pensée et machine*, Editions Champ Vallon, Seyssel, 1983.

SALLANTIN J., SZCZECINIARZ J.-J., *Le Concept de preuve à la lumière de l'intelligence artificielle*, Presses Universitaires de France, Paris, 1999.

GANASCIA J.-G., *L'âme-machine, les enjeux de lintelligence artificielle*, Le Seuil, Paris, 1990.

Popular science

TISSEAU G., PITRAT J., *Intelligence artificielle : problèmes et méthodes*, Presses Universitaires de France, Paris, 1996.

CREVIER D., BUKCEK N., *À la recherche de l'intelligence artificielle*, Flammarion, Paris, 1997.

CHALLONER J., *L'Intelligence artificielle : Un guide d'initiation au futur de l'informatique et de la robotique*, Pearson Education, New York, 2003.

BERSINI H., *De l'intelligence humaine à l'intelligence artificielle*, Ellipses, Paris, 2006.

Glossary

– **Artificial Intelligence**: Set of theories and techniques used to create machines capable of simulating intelligence.

– **BI**: Business Intelligence, all the tools and organization related to data management and exploitation for operational or analytical (decisional) purposes.

– **Big Data**: The "raw" data and all other types of data, which by definition exceed the "normal" data management capacity of a company (usually because of volume, velocity, variety...).

– **Data**: Information, raw material, the basic element of the information cycle.

– **Data Lake**: Database (or data storage warehouse) that contains data of any format, including structuring at the time of reading.

– **Deep Learning**: Extension of Machine Learning that incorporates supervised learning and self-learning functions based on complex, multidimensional data representation models.

– **DataMART**: Subject-oriented decision database (specialized for a domain). For example, a "customer" DataMART would be a decision database specifically designed for customer relations management.

– **Data Warehouse**: Decision-making database that contains all the company's decision-making data (all subjects).

– **Expert systems**: AI systems based on high-level knowledge modeling with predicate logics (if this then that, that this is in that, etc.) and rules engines.

– **GAFA**: Acronym for Google, Apple, Facebook and Amazon (the main online actors).

– **Hadoop**: Set of Big Data processing processes and techniques.

– **Machine Learning**: AI technique allowing problems of environment perception (visual, audio, etc.) to be solved in a more efficient way than with traditional procedural algorithms. It is often based on the use of artificial neural networks.

– **Neural networks**: AI technique that simulates the functioning of neural cells to reproduce the functioning of the human brain. Mainly used in speech and image recognition. It can be simulated through software or with specialized electronic circuits.

– **Rules engines**: Technical solutions enabling the implementation of expert systems and exploiting predicate databases (rules).

   – Strong Artificial Intelligence: Produces intelligent behavior but is also able to experience self-consciousness or "feelings", which means having an understanding and reasoning.

   – Weak Artificial Intelligence: This is more about the engineering of a system that tries to be autonomous and the algorithms solve problems.

Index

Advances in Information Systems Set

coordinated by Camille Rosenthal-Sabroux

Other titles from

in

Information Systems, Web and Pervasive Computing

2017

BOUHAÏ Nasreddine, SALEH Imad
Internet of Things: Evolutions and Innovations
(Digital Tools and Uses Set – Volume 4)

DUONG Véronique
Baidu SEO: Challenges and Intricacies of Marketing in China

LESAS Anne-Marie, MIRANDA Serge
The Art and Science of NFC Programming
(Intellectual Technologies Set – Volume 3)

LIEM André
Prospective Ergonomics
(Human-Machine Interaction Set – Volume 4)

MARSAULT Xavier
Eco-generative Design for Early Stages of Architecture
(Architecture and Computer Science Set – Volume 1)

REYES-GARCIA Everardo
The Image-Interface: Graphical Supports for Visual Information
(Digital Tools and Uses Set – Volume 3)

REYES-GARCIA Everardo, BOUHAÏ Nasreddine
Designing Interactive Hypermedia Systems
(Digital Tools and Uses Set – Volume 2)

SAÏD Karim, BAHRI KORBI Fadia
Asymmetric Alliances and Information Systems:Issues and Prospects
(Advances in Information Systems Set – Volume 7)

SZONIECKY Samuel, BOUHAÏ Nasreddine
Collective Intelligence and Digital Archives: Towards Knowledge
Ecosystems
(Digital Tools and Uses Set – Volume 1)

2016

BEN CHOUIKHA Mona
Organizational Design for Knowledge Management

BERTOLO David
Interactions on Digital Tablets in the Context of 3D Geometry Learning
(Human-Machine Interaction Set – Volume 2)

BOUVARD Patricia, SUZANNE Hervé
Collective Intelligence Development in Business

EL FALLAH SEGHROUCHNI Amal, ISHIKAWA Fuyuki, HÉRAULT Laurent,
TOKUDA Hideyuki
Enablers for Smart Cities

FABRE Renaud, in collaboration with MESSERSCHMIDT-MARIET Quentin,
HOLVOET Margot
New Challenges for Knowledge

GAUDIELLO Ilaria, ZIBETTI Elisabetta
Learning Robotics, with Robotics, by Robotics
(Human-Machine Interaction Set – Volume 3)

HENROTIN Joseph
The Art of War in the Network Age
(Intellectual Technologies Set – Volume 1)

KITAJIMA Munéo
Memory and Action Selection in Human–Machine Interaction
(Human–Machine Interaction Set – Volume 1)

LAGRAÑA Fernando
E-mail and Behavioral Changes: Uses and Misuses of Electronic Communications

LEIGNEL Jean-Louis, UNGARO Thierry, STAAR Adrien
Digital Transformation
(Advances in Information Systems Set – Volume 6)

NOYER Jean-Max
Transformation of Collective Intelligences
(Intellectual Technologies Set – Volume 2)

VENTRE Daniel
Information Warfare – 2nd edition

VITALIS André
The Uncertain Digital Revolution

2015

ARDUIN Pierre-Emmanuel, GRUNDSTEIN Michel, ROSENTHAL-SABROUX Camille
Information and Knowledge System
(Advances in Information Systems Set   Volume 2)

BÉRANGER Jérôme
Medical Information Systems Ethics

BRONNER Gérald
Belief and Misbelief Asymmetry on the Internet

IAFRATE Fernando
From Big Data to Smart Data
(Advances in Information Systems Set – Volume 1)

KRICHEN Saoussen, BEN JOUIDA Sihem
Supply Chain Management and its Applications in Computer Science

LEBRATY Jean-Fabrice, LOBRE-LEBRATY Katia
Crowdsourcing: One Step Beyond

SALLABERRY Christian
Geographical Information Retrieval in Textual Corpora

2012

BUCHER Bénédicte, LE BER Florence
Innovative Software Development in GIS

GAUSSIER Eric, YVON François
Textual Information Access

STOCKINGER Peter
Audiovisual Archives: Digital Text and Discourse Analysis

VENTRE Daniel
Cyber Conflict

2011

BANOS Arnaud, THÉVENIN Thomas
Geographical Information and Urban Transport Systems

DAUPHINÉ André
Fractal Geography

LEMBERGER Pirmin, MOREL Mederic
Managing Complexity of Information Systems

STOCKINGER Peter
Introduction to Audiovisual Archives

STOCKINGER Peter
Digital Audiovisual Archives

VENTRE Daniel
Cyberwar and Information Warfare

2010

BONNET Pierre
Enterprise Data Governance

BRUNET Roger
Sustainable Geography

CARREGA Pierre
Geographical Information and Climatology

CAUVIN Colette, ESCOBAR Francisco, SERRADJ Aziz
Thematic Cartography – 3-volume series
Thematic Cartography and Transformations – Volume 1
Cartography and the Impact of the Quantitative Revolution – Volume 2
New Approaches in Thematic Cartography – Volume 3

LANGLOIS Patrice
Simulation of Complex Systems in GIS

MATHIS Philippe
Graphs and Networks – 2nd edition

THERIAULT Marius, DES ROSIERS François
Modeling Urban Dynamics

2009

BONNET Pierre, DETAVERNIER Jean-Michel, VAUQUIER Dominique
Sustainable IT Architecture: the Progressive Way of Overhauling Information Systems with SOA

PAPY Fabrice
Information Science

RIVARD François, ABOU HARB Georges, MERET Philippe
The Transverse Information System

ROCHE Stéphane, CARON Claude
Organizational Facets of GIS

2008

BRUGNOT Gérard
Spatial Management of Risks

FINKE Gerd
Operations Research and Networks

GUERMOND Yves
Modeling Process in Geography

KANEVSKI Michael
Advanced Mapping of Environmental Data

MANOUVRIER Bernard, LAURENT Ménard
Application Integration: EAI, B2B, BPM and SOA

PAPY Fabrice
Digital Libraries

2007

DOBESCH Hartwig, DUMOLARD Pierre, DYRAS Izabela
Spatial Interpolation for Climate Data

SANDERS Lena
Models in Spatial Analysis

2006

CLIQUET Gérard
Geomarketing

CORNIOU Jean-Pierre
Looking Back and Going Forward in IT

DEVILLERS Rodolphe, JEANSOULIN Robert
Fundamentals of Spatial Data Quality

Printed and bound by CPI Group (UK) Ltd, Croydon, CR0 4YY